mountain
bike guide

C000246557

North Wales

2012

Pete Bursnall

www.ernest-press.co.uk

First published by The Ernest Press 1995
Reprinted with Addendum 2002
© Pete Bursnall
This second edition was written by Pete and completed by Matt Strickland   2012

ISBN 978 0 948153 99 0

British Library Cataloguing-in-Publication Data has been registered with the British
Library in Wetherby and is available on request.

Typeset by JAC creative
Printed by Martins the Printers

© Crown Copyright and/or database right. All rights reserved. Licence number
100053017

Whilst we have made every effort to achieve accuracy in producing the routes in this
guidebook, the authors, publishers & copyright owners can take no responsibility for
trespass, irresponsible riding, or loss or damage to persons or property suffered as a
result of the route descriptions in this guide.

Inclusion of a route in this guide does not guarantee that it will remain a right of
way. If conflict with a landowner occurs, please be polite and leave by the shortest
possible route – then check the situation with the relevant authority.

It is emphasised that riders must give way to pedestrians and horse riders, and should
make every effort to warn others of their approach.

Readers are reminded that mountain biking is an inherently dangerous activity.

Contents

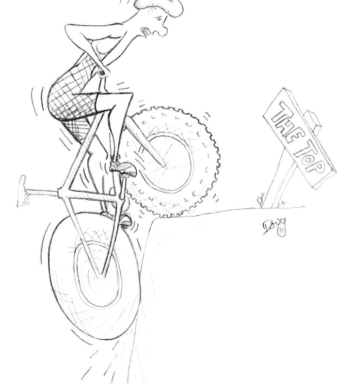

Routes

Bike Fever

(With apologies to John Masefield)

I must go out on my bike again, to the lonely road and the trail
And all I ask is a good bike and the route laid out like Braille
And the gear's click and the tyre's hum and the long road snaking
And a grey mist on the Stig's face as I cruise past overtaking.

I must go out on my bike again for the call of the evening ride
It's a wild call and a clear call that may not be denied
And all I ask is a windless day with sunshine smiling
And the long day and the big climbs with the road bike flying.

I must go out on my bike again, to the vagrant gypsy life
To the road's way and the trail's way where the climb's like a whetted knife
And all I ask is a merry yarn from a laughing fellow rider
And a quiet tea and a sticky cake when the long hard ride is over.

Matt Strickland.

Introduction

Back in '91 and '95 when I wrote my Mid and North Wales Guides I never
thought for even a moment that I would be back in 2009/11 rewriting them
both. Neither did I foresee how mountain biking would develop and mature over
the coming years; growing into an activity tourism staple, spawning sub genres,
international competitions, multinational organisations and purpose-built facilities.
Back then it was just the natural development of what we had done as kids: fit cow
horn handlebars to old bikes, push them up hills then race them down again with
little control and even less braking power.

Coming from a touring background, the mountain bike was a great enabler, allowing access to places other bikes could never reach. They allow areas to be linked up, journeys to develop and adventures to be had, in the same way that sea kayaks and Para gliders have for me in other media. I rode my first one, a Yeti competition bike, while on a climbing trip to Chamonix in '86; I had never seen anything like it; neither had my mates when I met them at the bus station, cooool!

In a similar way the new Ordnance Survey 'Explorer' maps have moved things on in terms of access. Now that there is a more complete listing of bridleways and byways a whole new raft of possibilities has been enabled, possibilities that did not exist when I wrote the first two books. As such it has been a pleasure to get back out there exploring on my bike, hours spent poring over maps, websites and Google Earth resulting in new routes, changed routes, better routes.

I make no excuse for my preference for routes that make sense both on the ground and on the map. I love exploring and the sense of moving through the environment as much as I enjoy the technical and physical aspects of mountain biking. There are twiddly bits that I could add in to some routes but these often look and feel contrived, just there to grab a few metres of singletrack or descent. I leave those for you to discover.

I also make no excuse for the fact that quite a few of the XC routes have varying amounts of road in them. In Northern Wales, unless you are at a trail centre, you will often need to join up sections of offroad by using minor roads etc. You can see this as a problem if you like but in reality it is just what needs to be done to get the best out of the riding environment. There are some routes with little or no road but if you stick to those routes then you will miss out on some amazing trails. Some of the roads are pretty breathtaking too, with wide views, and where possible I have tried to ride up a road and down offroad.

I have grown frustrated by the trend in some guidebooks for the route descriptions to be reduced to a bare minimum of statistics and a bunch of over excited adjectives, which in the end, add little to informing the rider what to expect on the trail. In order to avoid this trap I have kept the route descriptions as clear as possible, but without sacrificing detail, whilst at the same time including some short ride stories by way of an extended introduction. These I hope will give a sense of what it is like to ride in a particular area, the look and feel of the trail and the area around it, environmental, physical and even sometimes spiritual aspect of the Northern Welsh mountains.

Equipment

Choice of MTB equipment is a very personal thing; what works for one may not work for others. On top of that we all have different ideas of just what kit is needed for a ride and how much emergency / spare gear to carry. Talk to other riders; learn from their experiences.

Just about every ride in this guide has been ridden on a ten year old, bog standard £500 Dawes 'Edge' steel framed hard-tail. For XC riding I prefer the stiffness of the frame, the fact that it is very efficient to pedal and that it is easily shouldered for carries. Over the last few thousand kilometres it has served me very well, never letting me down, though it is now at least 25% new parts and 25% recycled parts from an aging Orange 'Clockwork'. The frame, wheels, chainrings, forks and headset are all original and deserving of respect given the huge amount of riding they have undertaken.

I also own a £600 from ebay Marin 'Attack Ridge' which I prefer for night-riding and trail centres. This is a much more aggressive bike with 130mm of travel at both ends and an aluminium frame. It gives a much smoother ride and more control on rocky and technical sections. Not so good for XC though given the slightly less efficient frame and very much less efficient tyres, not to mention that it is a nightmare to carry.

For the road rides I have a Scott CR1 Pro Carbon, a gorgeous bit of technology / art that weighs less than my breakfast and responds like a slapped stallion.

Buying a bike is all about doing your research, riding other people's bikes then finding one on ebay! If you don't 'have to have' this year's model with its 'ever so slightly better' design then you can often pick up a great bike for half price online. For the £2k that seems to get you a standard bike these days you can get a full quiver of second hand bikes but make sure you do your research first. My experience is that it is legs and lungs that have the biggest effect on your performance and not the age of your bike.

Tom Carter carting his bike! Bwlch Cwm Llan.

My choice of clothing comes from decades as an outdoor person and knowing that 1) you get what you pay for and 2) different disciplines do often need specifically designed clothing. You can get by with clothes taken from climbing or walking or kayaking but if you spend a lot of time on your bike you will appreciate the subtleties of specially designed kit.

The vast majority of my clothes are made by Endura, well thought out and well made by people who understand the rider's needs. The combinations of shorts, tights, gloves, undershirts, jackets etc for different weathers is infinite and depends on your physiology. I have suffered from skin cancer so my summer wear is a lightweight long-sleeved jersey, three quarter tights and a gilet stuffed into a pocket. The shoulders of the season see a proper Goretex jacket, baggies and a short-sleeved thermal added to the list. The winter can be anything in this country but in extremes I use a Merino wool undershirt and waterproof tights, both of which are blissful bits of kit. I also have an ancient but cosy Thermofleece roadie jumper that gets dragged out in foul weather. I was so pleased with my Endura kit that I hunted them down as sponsors so that I could get more.

All my bikes have clipless pedals or SPD's, which are worn loose on the mountain bikes and tight on the road bike. I have basic Shimano MO76 summer shoes which last about a season and their winter MW80 shoe for the cold and wet season. I also have some neoprene over-booties for the in-between times. Buying shoes and boots can be a nightmare, the best deals being online, but relative shoe sizes vary and so I have stuck with one brand that I trust and know what size fits.

My toolkit is stuffed into a Camelbak hydration rucksack and consists of all the things I have broken and wished I carried over the years: plus the tools to use them. Chain links, spare cleats for my shoes, brake and gear cables, a few nuts 'n' bolts and a couple of inner tubes as well as various puncture repair kits, allen keys, tyre levers, a penknife, adjustable spanner, chain splitter, pliers, screwdriver etc. When I am out with friends then one of us will have a first-aid kit. If I am on my own then I don't bother; my choice.

I have had a few 'moments' during the riding for this guide, most notably a puncture coupled with a broken pump when 20km from home (ten minutes of worried fiddling with the pump to get it sort-of working) and exploding disk brakes at the top of a huge hill making for a very slow and extremely frustrating descent. Everything else I have sorted easily or lived with until I got back. I service my bikes after every ride and never jet wash them. You have to be mad to blow high pressure water at your precious bearings, though it probably keeps the bike shop guys happy. Low pressure water to get the worst of the mud off, degreaser and a rag to clean the drive system followed by WD40 on mechanicals to push out moisture and thin oil on the chain. After that it's tweak the gears and set up the bike for the next ride. Anything that may be on its way out is pre-emptively replaced so as to avoid disasters where possible. From time to time I take the bikes to Evolution Cycles in Bangor for a pro service. I can tell the difference despite having fiddled with bikes for years.

My worst cock-up was to change the chain but not the cassette just before a night ride. As soon as we started riding the gears were jumping all over and I almost gave up before finding that the two biggest cogs worked with the smallest chainring. I then spent the next two hours spinning like a dervish at the back of the pack, lesson learnt.

I drink Maximuscle energy and recovery 'Viper' carbohydrate drink before and after rides to maintain my salts and minerals as well as to aid recovery. I think it makes a difference, especially if you ride for several days on the trot. During a ride I drink water and eat home-made flapjack and dried fruit.

Maps are always the OS 1:25,000 variety and I have learnt the hard way that it is worth spending the extra money on the waterproof versions. There is nothing worse than being a long way from home in crappy weather holding the bits of a soggy map soup.

Got a head? Get a helmet. Got eyes? Get eye protection.

Riding Tips

During the research for this guide I have fallen off and crashed more times than I like to remember. Most have been fairly innocuous slips but one or two have been proper crashes that could have resulted in some serious injuries. I was lucky and only gathered a few big bruises and some nasty cuts. I noticed that there were a few themes to these events. Maybe it was me, maybe it's the type of riding I do, either way the top causes of inelegant dismounts were:

1) **Getting rutted.** Catching either the pedal or wheel on the side wall of a rut resulting in getting thrown over sideways. The best technique I found (apart from avoiding the rut in the first place) was to put a lot of weight onto the offside handlebar to lean the bike away from the side of the rut. Turning the front wheel does not work as the trailing edge of the front wheel clatters along the edge of the rut and you just get shaken about then off you come. You have to be quick but it does work.

2) **Nasty slabs.** Sloping slabs of smooth bedrock that go either across or along the trail, or in the worst case both, can be very tricky in the wet. The best thing to do is to take the fall line if possible, get lined up early and let the bike roll until you get off the other end or reach a rougher section of the slab where there is more grip. Often there is a bit of a gully around the lower edge of the slab where water runs and this can sometimes give a sneaky route. Good tyres help and sometimes leaning the bike a bit to keep it perpendicular to the ground can help avoid the instantaneous, ice rink dismount.

3) **Loose rocks.** One of the big differences between wild and manufactured riding is the looseness of the trails. In the wild you will come across descents where there are loose rocks of all sizes that move about or jump from under your wheels as you descend. On manufactured trails they tend to be bedded in, big rock gardens but solid. Going too slowly on loose descents causes the bike to 'push the rocks around' with the front wheel whereas a bit more speed allows you to flow over them. Coming off the front brake lifts the nose of the bike allowing an over rather

than through attitude; digging in with the brakes does just that. Speed is your friend!

4) Drop offs. Coming down a slope to be faced with a step can be a bit scary and the instinctive reaction is to grab some brake lever. This can result in you stopping the front wheel as you go 'over the top' and then landing on a locked wheel very close to the base of the drop giving the steepest bike angle possible. Better to use only a little front brake and more back in this instance, better still is to let the bike roll so that the front wheel lands as far in front of the step as possible to flatten the drop out. The really good riders land both wheels at the same time having lifted the front wheel and let the bike roll freely over the step; takes a bit of skill and courage to do well. From both the last two paragraphs you can see that it is important to know when to let the bike run a bit, but...

5) Too much speed. Ok we all do it, the red mist descends and off we go, yeehaaa! The only cure is great brakes, good reactions and a little bit of caution on unknown trails. We are all going to get bitten at some point, better get used to the idea.

6) Line choice. Good line choice is a key skill, reading the trail ahead and either avoiding or attacking the challenges that you see approaching. Looking a good way ahead allows you to set the right speed, correct gear and best approach to the next section of trail; proactive riding. The closer to the front wheel that you are looking the more reactive you have to be, the bike gets twitchy and you tense up. Sometimes you get locked in to looking only a few feet in front of the wheel, or worse, survival mode! This feels bad as you have no idea what is ahead and frequently miss the good line by fixating on each rock or drop as it appears in your small sphere of vision. The best thing is often to either stop and refocus or be brave, let go of the brakes a bit, lift your eyes from the floor and look ahead.

If you are coming off then I have found two ways of doing it depending on the crash. For a low speed sideways fall I tend to unclip the downhill foot but keep it off the ground trying to place it about a metre away from the bike. This means that the cross bar does not come down on my leg to knock me over; I am more stable and can let the bike drop to the floor whilst remaining upright.

For the full on wipe-out I just try to get away from the bike, tuck a shoulder under and land on my camelback! Roll Charlie Brown Roll! The only bone I have broken on a bike was my scaphoid (in the wrist) and that was as a result of putting my hand out in front of me during a crash.

Lastly it is important to get off the saddle when descending or travelling on rough ground of any angle, letting the bike move around under you by supplementing its suspension with your own, your arms and legs. This means that your body stays relatively still while the bike bucks about allowing you to soak up the bumps and keep your vision clear. Dropping the saddle for long tricky descents is a good idea and gives even more ability to move about. You can also pump the bike over the bumps and berms to keep the bike's speed up rather than having to pedal all the time. Active riding rules; don't be a passenger on your own bike.

Bike shops

Beics Beddgelert, The Bike Barn, Beddgelert Forest, LL55 4UU, 01766 890 434
Beics Betws, Betws y Coed, LL24 0AB, 01690 710 766
Beics Brenin, Coed y Brenin Visitor Centre, LL40 2HZ, 01341 440 728
Beics Menai,1 Slate Quay, Caernarfon, LL55 2PB, 01286 676 804
Bike Shop, Stansty Road, Wrexham, LL11 2HR, 01978 354 429
Cellar Cycles, 5 Well St. Ruthin, LL15 1AE, 01824 707133
Dolgellau Cycles, The Old Furnace, Dolgellau, LL40 1DE, 01341 423 332
Llanberis Bike Hire, Can y Ddraig, 34 High Street, Llanberis, LL55 4EU, 01286 872 787
One Planet Adventure, Coed Llandegla, LL11 3AA, 01978 751 656
Evolution Cycles, 141 High Street, Bangor, LL57 1NT, 01248 355 770
Rhroberts Cycles, High Street, Bala, 01678 520 252
Summit Cycles, 65 North Parade, Aberystwyth,SY23 2JN, 01970 626 061

The Holey Trail, 31 Maengwyn Road, Machynlleth, SY20 8EB, 01654 700 411
West End Cycles, 121 -127 Conway Rd, Llandudno, LL31 9BA, 01492 530 269

Acknowledgments

This book would not have been possible without the unending support of my wife Aila and kids; Owen and Riannon, thanks gang!

It would not have been as unhurried without the cover provided by the school gate team, Granny Barbara, Georgie Dearden, Leila Mapp and Dee Edwards.

Thanks to Wojciech Zedebsky for photographs and Paul Sandham for help with the mapping.

It would not have been as much fun without the company and conversation of an interesting bunch of riders, Matt and Åsa Strickland, Ash Charlwood, John Gladston, Paul Pritchard, Huw Verity, Alan Williams, Phil Oliver, Tristan O'Meara, Phil Goodman, Ali 'The Stig' Chant, James Camis, Lloyd Entwistle, Owen Bursnall, Leo Dearden, Tom Jones, Martin Williamson, Mal Grace, Tim Hall, Steffan Owen, Tom Carter, Sue Williams, June Riley, Craig Rockliff, John Jones, Dave Liddy and Andy Braund.

It would not have been as comfortable without the assistance of Endura UK.

It would not have been as trouble free without the help of Dawes Cycles.

It would not have been as slick without the services by Evolution Bikes.

I would also like to thank the people who buy £2000 bikes and then sell them a few months later on ebay for less than half that, without them I would have less bikes and less money.

Coedty Reservoir, the Cwm Eigiau route skirts the shore and the Carneddau Round climbs steeply above to eventually reach Llyn Cowlyd.

Carneddau (Capel Curig & Llanrwst)

INTRODUCTION - Crafnant Loop with Matt & James. (See map for ROUTE 01)

Sunday 19th April '09 - This morning I was off out with Matt and James for a roll around the lower slopes of the Carneddau. This loop is only 25 / 28 km depending on which way you start but it has the feel of a much longer ride. It is a bit of a killer loop, views to die for, tough technical sections and some strenuous climbing.

I rode this way 'on me tod' a couple of weeks ago but today I was in company in the hope of getting some good photos for the guide. The weather was perfect so failure to procure said images would rest on my shoulders alone.

Last time I took the shorter route, today we would take the longer and theoretically easier start. This heads up the old A5 from Capel Curig as far as the campsite, a short section back along the new A5 and then up onto the hills.

The guys then opted for the 'even easier' quasi legal (at least in Matt's mind) track while I followed the letter of the law across the moor. Sometimes the law is an ass and this is probably one of those times. Choose a rocky and indestructible track followed by a well made embankment or a muddy, grassy bog with a lost 'n' found bridleway that cuts up and damages easily, which one is most sustainable? Still, best to stick to the rights of way.

I got a good workout and we met up after a few minutes and got a couple of good pics. Strangely the longer ride seemed to offer harder work, despite the lower average angle. The shorter, more direct route has easier navigation and better, easier riding, especially now the moor has had all its ditches bridged by the nice people from the Uplands Footpath Trust.

The section along the Llyn Cowlyd is great, 'natural' singletrack is just so much more random and so much less predictable than the manufactured stuff. This makes for some extremely technical riding where getting the right gearing, line, speed and bike position are crucial. The further ahead you can plan the better and a splatter of aggression at the right time makes all the difference. Some of the drop offs are big and nasty, on steep ground with sharp rocks all around.

Up and over to Trefriw is all tarmac but the descent is a disc brake melting, blind bending, pray no cars are coming the other way, mouthwatering epic. The kind you just want to do again but there is no way on earth you would pedal back up, way too physical, and there just might be some nutter like you flying down the other way...

The long easy climb up to Llyn Crafnant feels like a rest after the last few km and the alpine scenery is almost enough to take your mind off any pain you may be feeling as you get into the spin of things along the road. The head of the Crafnant valley is more Lake District than the Lake District, a secret part of Snowdonia. Awkward to access by road it is therefore nowhere near as busy as the quality of the environment would suggest it should be.

Plenty of time to soak the ambiance in as you carry up the grassy path to the col and plenty of incentive to put all that to the back of your mind as you hit the most consistently technical riding of the day on it's far side. This is cruelly delivered at the time when you are at your most tired but a few seconds of rocky jarring sets the adrenaline to work and the weariness falls away, or you fall off, a lot. The best technical riding outside of a trail centre? It's a toss up between this and the Rhyd Ddu path on Snowdon.

The descent keeps working all the way down to Capel Curig, punctuated only by the odd flowing section and cheery greetings directed at the walkers that step aside to let us pass, or vice versa. This ride is one of the high points of mountain biking in these parts but one that you have to earn the right to enjoy. Take it on too soon, not fit enough, not dialed-in enough and you will get round for sure, but it will be survival, not pleasure. You will be glad to reach the end of it rather than wishing you were back at the beginning with fresh legs, ready to go again.

We were spoilt on our descent as we gratefully received extra supplies, delivered at a secret location known only to Matt's young sons. Rice salad, scandinavian olive mix thing and apple crumble, oh the hardship!

ROUTE 01 - Circuit of the Carneddau

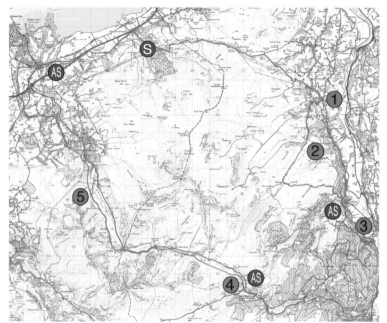

Gradient profile

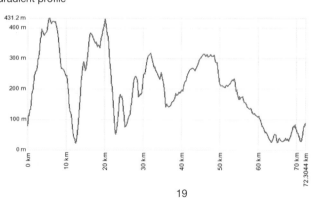

19

ROUTE 01 DETAILS (Circuit of the Carneddou)

Length:	78km
Height gain:	2000m
Difficulty:	Red
Commitment:	4
Stars:	★ ★
Map:	OL 17

ROUTE SUMMARY

A mammoth undertaking, with huge amounts of climb, not for the faint-hearted. There are a couple of 'save yourself a few kilometres' shortcuts and various options for finishing but nothing that will save you if you blow up. Most of the climbing is in the first half where three big climbs come one after the other in short order; steep would be an understatement. There is a fair bit of road needed to join the dots but there is also high and remote riding in very fine positions. The trails are made up of rocky tracks, grassy trails, part of the Marin, minor roads and cyclepaths. There are a number of cafes on or very near the route to keep the fires stoked. The best start is made from the linear carpark on the old road in Abergwyngregyn, GR 656

728, as this gives the easier riding at the end. Alternative starts abound: Bryn Glo, Capel Curig, Trefriw, Ogwen, Bangor, Bethesda... it's a long ride. A great day out, if you can get round.

Start from the carpark in Abergwyngregyn, GR 656 728, work your way through the village following the 'Aber Falls' signs then climb gently beside the river to reach a small carpark at a bridge. Go over the bridge to begin the first long climb out of the valley; continue up until you reach the end of the road. Go through the gate to join the rough track beyond and continue on this, climbing continuously as the views expand. After a level section you go through a couple of gates and the track becomes a road once more at GR 720 715. Follow this as it begins to descend into the Conwy Valley giving some enjoyable and fast minor road riding until it comes out at a T junction on the B5106, GR 767 689. Point 1.

Turn right but only for a couple of hundred yards, cross the Afon Dulyn then take the first right on another minor road. Climb this very steep road for about a kilometre and a half until it is possible to take the first road on the left, up then down through a gate to the end of the road at GR 757 668. Keep going on the rough track then continue in the same vein going left at the fork next to the 'no motors' road sign. Climb this steep and tricky track, through a gate then up the hillside high above Coedty Reservoir. This is an entertaining and stiff climb but completely rideable bar about 20m. Finally the climb ends at a gate on the shoulder of Moel Eilio with wide and impressive views and a track junction, GR 754 660. Point 2.

Take the right hand option following the good track towards Llyn Cowlyd. The line of the byway (as marked on the map) lies a little below the track having diverged a few hundred metres after the junction. There is little to see on the ground and a fence is reached with no gate, forcing you back up to the track to avoid crossing the fence. At about GR 747 650 the byway goes under the huge obstruction that is the hydro water pipe for Dolgarrog hydro station; surely this is an illegally blocked byway?! The best crossing point is just below a small ruin on the side of the track. Here it is possible to get under the pipe where a small stream goes under. Drop down to the obvious track to turn right. The byway once again diverges from the track to cut a corner before rejoining it very quickly. From there follow the track through gates and just below the pipe to reach a track junction. Go left and descend to the road at a small bridge, GR 745 641.

Climb away from the bridge following the steep road to the shoulder of Cefn Cyfarwydd before enjoying a monumental road descent to the outskirts of Trefriw. At the T junction, GR 778 632. Go right then first left to quickly engage with yet another steep climb. This one leads up through trees to reach the hamlet of Llanrhychwyn where you make a left turn to descend (mostly) to a T junction in the forest at GR 789 609. Point 3.

Directly opposite is the 'Saw Bench' carpark where the Marin Trail begins. Go into the carpark and join the Marin. Follow the Marin through 'Pigs might fly', 'Blue', 'Pandora's Rocks', 'Cyffty Tube', 'Sleepy Bear' and finally 'Dragon's Tail' to emerge onto a road (where the Marin goes straight over) at GR 758 579. Turn right, dropping down a steep narrow road to emerge at the A5 next to the 'Ugly House'.

Cross the bridge to the left then make a right turn onto a minor road. Follow this quiet lane for a few kilometres until it rejoins the A5 at Pont Cyfyng and you go left (Bryn Glo café 100m to the right). Time for a quick dash along the A5 through Capel Curig, luckily most of this section is in a 30mph limit. Keep going until you reach the junction next to the Pinnacle Café where you should leave the main road, crossing to the minor lane that leads to Joe Brown's and the small village carpark & toilets, GR 720 582. Point 4.

Ride straight past the carpark continuing along the track when the

tarmac ends. This is the old A5 and it leads you through the first half of the Ogwen Valley, traffic free, with great mountain views. You emerge briefly at Gwern y Gof Isaf (camping), pass in front of the farm then go straight over the access road, back onto the obvious line of the old road. More of the same until you are forced back onto the new A5 just under the slopes of Tryfan. You have 2km of this road to do; there is a cycleway marked on the northern side for much of the way but beware narrow sections facing the oncoming traffic and some uncertainty as to just where the cycleway becomes pavement.

At Idwal Cottage make a left turn past the carparks (tea shack) onto a minor lane which runs on the opposite side of the valley to the A5, GR 649 603. This gives more or less traffic free riding in a fine position until it is possible to join Lon Las Ogwen Cycleway by going straight on through the gate when the road goes right, GR 630 637, not where it is marked on some older maps. Point 5.

Follow the enjoyable cycleway, crossing the odd road until you emerge onto the B4409 at GR 615 664. Turn left along the road for a couple of kilometres until you have descended through Tregarth. Keep an eye out for signs for the cycleway on your left, there are a couple of entries and they are easily missed at speed. Drop onto the old railway line (cycleway) then cross on the new bridge over the busy B4366 back onto the railway on the opposite side. Belt along this, emerging to pass under the A55 then back along the railway.

You are now looking for an obvious left turn just before a bridge arch, GR 587 706. Go left here but then immediately right and over the bridge. Follow this lane to a roundabout next to the entrance to Penrhyn Castle. You want to go more or less straight over but need to dog-leg a little to do it. Follow the road past Tal y Bont, keeping to the road until it bears right to join the A55. At that point make a left to access the bridge over the trunk road. Once over the bridge make another left then follow this lane as it gently climbs away from the valley bottom. Follow this lane with some nice descending bends all the way back to Abergwyngregyn and the end of the route.

Top of the long initial climb on the Marin Trail.

ROUTE 02 - Cwm Eigiau

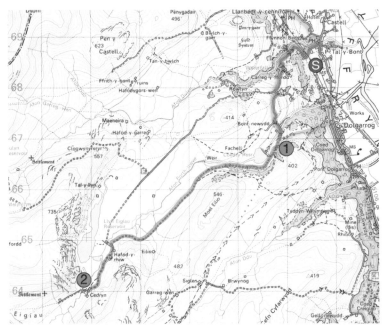

Gradient profile

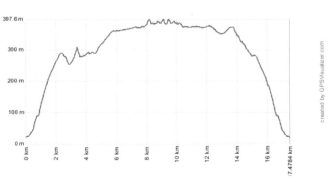

ROUTE 02 DETAILS - Cwm Eigiau

Length:	18km
Height gain:	600m
Difficulty:	Red
Commitment:	3
Stars:	★
Map:	OL / Explorer 17

ROUTE SUMMARY

A bit of an oddity as this is a 'there and back' ride and contains the mother of all road climbs to start the ride, yuk. The payback is some pleasant riding high up above Llyn Eigiau and close-up views of the mountains in a quiet spot. Start from any of the roadside parking in Tal y Bont / Dolgarrog, GR 767 687. There is a pub right at the bottom of the route, does a decent pint.

From wherever you are parked find the lane leading up the southern side of Afon Dulyn, GR 766 688, the first house up the lane is Yr Hen Felin. Climb the lane as it gets progressively steeper, there are views but you won't see them. The worst is over after about 2.2km where you reach a junction and must turn left, still climbing but not much. Drop down to reach the end of the road a short way after a gate and passing under the pipeline taking water down to what is now Dolgarrog Hydro station. Point 1.

Climb up a short way before taking the right-hand track through a gate and along the edge of the Coedty Reservoir. The left-hand track leads steeply up and over to the Cowlyd Reservoir, another day maybe, more climbing definitely.

Follow the track now for several kilometres of relatively flat pedaling, though the trail is often wet and grassy. Make the most of the view and choose whether to risk the old bridges or take the bypasses. After four kilometres or so you arrive at the wall of the dam, now punctured and ruined after tragically bursting in November 1925 causing 16 deaths in the valley below.

Go left around the edge of the dam wall before taking a narrow bridge off to the right when the good track heads uphill to a house in some trees. Follow this rough and slippy trail with the required concentration until you reach the very end of the bridleway where it heads over to a house (Cedryn) in the valley floor, GR 719 640. Point 2. If you have the inclination it is well worth an hour to leave the bikes here before walking up the track to the upper cwm nestled under the cliffs of Pen yr Helig Ddu. If not then it is time to retrace your steps back to the Conwy Valley some 400m of altitude below. Have a care on the descent though as the road is blind, narrow and some of the corners tighten up.

The end of the road, from here we walk, Cwm Eigiau route.

ROUTE 03 - Druids and Romans

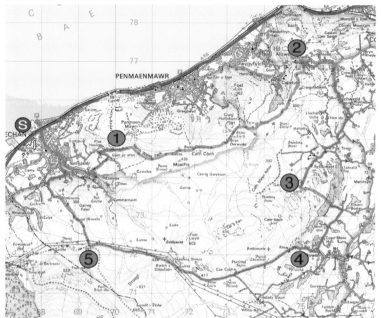

Gradient profile

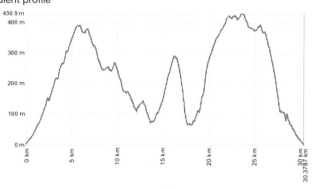

created by GPSVisualizer.com

27

ROUTE 03 DETAILS - Druids and Romans

Length:	30km
Height gain:	1100m
Difficulty:	Red/Black
Commitment:	3
Stars:	★ ★ ★
Map:	OL / Explorer 17

ROUTE SUMMARY

This strenuous route makes the best possible 'circumnavigation' of parts of the Carneddau. Three long climbs, some great descending, interesting navigation, wide views and the feeling of being a long way from home make this a route not to be taken lightly. One of the best routes in the guide, only 30km but feeling somewhat longer. If facilities were not an issue it is possible to start from any of the Sychnant carparks (near Point 2) which would allow you to 'cut the tail off' the section through Llanfairfechan saving about 4km and some ascent, but then you would not have started from the sea.

Climb number one. Start from the carpark on the front at Llanfairfechan, GR 678 755, then head up the hill, under the A55 and coast railway to the crossroads and traffic lights. Go straight over at the lights continuing up through the shops etc until the road bears right over a bridge. At this point make a left turn to follow this road uphill through more houses until you reach a point at GR 698 741 where the road once more bears right over a bridge but you go straight on climbing steeply round to the left past the country park and into open countryside.

This road leads up then around to the left with fine sea views until it is possible to take the first right turn near a house with pointed roofs at GR 695 746. Making sure you take the first available right, climb steeply up the road until it becomes a track bearing left towards the quarry; at this point go straight on through the gate towards a farm. The grassy path through the farm leads on to an energetic climb onto the open hillside through a number of gates. Getting back down the right way from here requires a little concentration… Point 1.

The track now leads you in a fine position close to a number of stone circles overlooking the sea. With the wall close on your left keep a lookout for a 'North Wales Path' marker in some rushes just where the track begins a straight climb. Follow the marker, a little vaguely at first, close to the wall and back onto an improving track first down and then up through a small col to the north of Cefn Coch, GR 726 747.

Drop enjoyably down the other side taking the track through a kissing gate leading towards a line of trees, then along the avenue in front of a house. Go through the new gate beyond the property then down beside a wall keeping your eye open for a tall marker post at a gate on the right. Screech to a halt to go through this then down the grassy path beyond.

50m beyond where the grassy path meets another you need to head left towards the obvious wall by going around a small lump. This section is vague for 100m or so but keep the wall close on your left and you will soon reach an old gate that leads down to a stream 30m beyond.

Cross the stream via the stepping stones then take the track through the bog keeping the wall a little way away on your left. The temptation is to head over to the wall but it is better to strike out through the middle of the bog as it soon dries out. The narrow trail then leads you easily over to the wall and a junction with another path that comes in from the right, GR 744 756. The section from here to the Sychnant Pass is delightful riding with wide views but is riddled with paths and tracks, some of which go the wrong way, some of the others are not rights of way etc.

Ride the main track in a fine position until you climb rockily; as the track bears right you take a gate and stile on your left leading into the 'Pensychnant

Nature Reserve'. Take this route up and over the lump, keeping an eye out for horses. Staying on the legal route takes a little concentration for the next few minutes but if you do get lost most routes end up in the same place, ish.

Once in the nature reserve, fork left, turn left, turn left again, bear right after the fast grassy descent, then go sharp left at the trees before finally passing through a gate onto the tarmac at the Sychnant Pass, GR 750 770 and relax! Point 2.

Climb up the tarmac then drop quickly down the far side to take a road junction on the right after about a kilometre all told. This narrow road leads you over and into the Conwy Valley, dropping steeply down to a T junction. Watch your speed though as there are a couple of holiday parks on the way.

Climb number two. At the T junction go right, climbing this road forsaking all others until you reach a junction with a phonebox and signposted Eglwys Llangelynnin. Go left climbing until you reach the end of the road near a farm, go straight on through the gate then onto the stony track beyond where a tidy driveway goes right, GR 749 737. Hopefully you have enough left in the tank to make it up the last loose challenge on the climb, if not then you are in for some fun later... Point 3.

Follow the walled track to the beautifully situated ancient church then continue in some style down the track as it gets steeper and more rocky before reaching the edge of Parc Mawr woods. Drop into the woods going straight over a junction then zigzagging down very, very steep and loose ground to reach the gate leading out of the bottom of the wood. Bear left descending to a junction, turn right to roll gently along the hillside above Rowen to a final tarmac junction where you should get into your lowest gear. Point 4.

Climb number three. Climb steeply, then climb more steeply, then push up to the YHA. Pass the hostel joining a rocky track leading onto the open hillside, gratefully accepting the easing of the angle. The track eventually reaches a road onto which you bear right heading up to Bwlch y Ddeufaen at GR 720 715. Join the Roman road cursing the pylons as they haunt you along the stunning track. At the signposted crossroads, Point 5, turn right towards Llanfairfechan dropping down the smooth grassy track. Keep on the main track until it leads you out onto an open hillside just beyond a wall. Bear left following the wall down the fast grass but beware mountain ponies and suicidal sheep as you flow down. Beware also the final 100m or so after a gate; desperate when wet and technical in the dry, this leads you to the tarmac at a gate beside a house.

Turn right and make a final climb around the back of the village to reach a point you will recognise from three climbs ago. Descend the road to a right turn at the T junction, go straight over the traffic lights and collapse onto the beach with a grin.

Huw Verity high above Penmaenmawr with the Great Orm below, Druids, Druids & Romans

31

ROUTE 04 - Druids

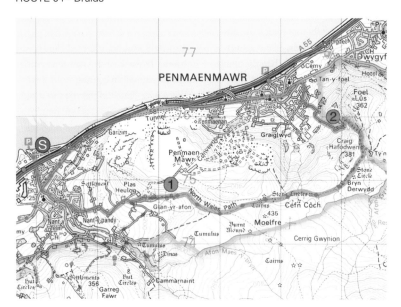

Gradient profile

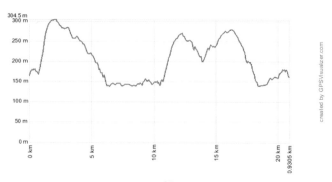

ROUTE 04 DETAILS - Druids

Length:	14km
Height gain:	500m
Difficulty:	Blue
Commitment:	1
Stars:	★
Map:	OL 17

ROUTE SUMMARY

This is the shortest ride in the guide and one that lends itself well to training rides or night rides (once you know the route) or even a quick filler when time is short. That said it still has a big 400m non-stop climb, great views and some fun trails to enjoy. Start from the seafront carpark in Llanfairfechan, GR 678 755.

Start from the carpark on the front at Llanfairfechan. Head up the hill, under the A55 and coast railway to the crossroads and traffic lights. Go straight over at the lights continuing up through the shops etc until the road bears right over a bridge. At this point make a left turn to follow this road uphill before taking the next left turn up 'Mount Road' rather than continuing along the 'Valley Road'.

Now get stuck in to a serious bit of tarmac climbing; expect no mercy and give none until there is a very short respite just before the next junction. Take the second left turn near a house with pointed roofs at GR 695 746. Making sure you take the second left as there are two together, climb steeply up the road until it becomes a track bearing left towards the quarry; at this point go straight on through the gate towards a farm. Point 1. Through the farm the grassy path leads to an energetic climb onto the open hillside through a number of gates. That's the climbing done, getting back down the right way from here requires a little concentration.

The track now leads you in a fine position close to a number of stone circles overlooking the sea. With the wall close on your left keep a lookout for a 'North Wales Path' marker in some rushes just where the track begins a straight climb. Follow the marker, a little vaguely at first, close to the wall and back onto an improving track. Follow this up to a small col to the north of Cefn Coch, GR 726 747.

Drop enjoyably down the other side taking the track through a gate and kissing gate leading towards a line of trees, then along the avenue in front of a house. Go through the new gate beyond the property then down the track beside a wall with speed and pleasure. Keep to this track as it leads you round the back of Foel Lus with sea views and increasing steepness. Bear left in front of some big stone 'gateposts' as the track becomes a road. Point 2. Shoot down this with care for up-coming traffic and the lack of width on the road.

Keep to the road bearing right at a junction where it is possible to go straight over via a bollarded lane (the road is better as it has less pedestrians)

then drop to a T junction with a bigger road. Go left then left again at the main Penmaenmawr town thoroughfare; follow this to the A55. Just as you think the dual carriageway is your route back bear sharp left behind a building then up a ramp leading to a bridge over the fast moving traffic. Follow this foot / cycleway above the road in an interesting position until it brings you back down in Llanfairfechan. Follow the 'Route 8' signs through the houses then down to the road through the village. Bear left along this, continuing until you reach the traffic lights where you go right and drop back to the beach front carpark.

ROUTE 05 - Llyn Anafon

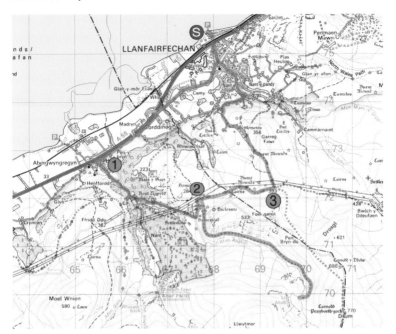

Gradient profile

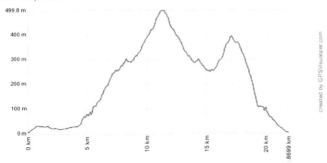

ROUTE 05 DETAILS - Llyn Anafon

Length:	22km
Height gain:	600m
Difficulty:	Red
Commitment:	2
Stars:	★ ★
Map:	OL / Explorer 17

ROUTE SUMMARY

An enjoyable route up to a remote reservoir followed by two winding descents, all undertaken in fine position once the initial but short section beside the A55 is completed. The riding is pretty straight-forward but the initial climb is very long and continuous. The central part of route is not a bridleway but the National Trust has agreed to allow mountain bikes on the well-made track to the lake provided that they are ridden responsibly. Should this situation change then please respect any signage etc that you may come across.

Start from the large free carpark right on the sea shore in Llanfairfechan, GR 678 754. From there head back into the village passing under the A55 trunk-road and the railway to reach a crossroads and traffic lights. Turn right here to follow the Aber Road pleasantly out of the village until just as it is about to cross and then join the A55 take a left turn down a smaller road Ffrodd Gwyllt running parallel to the trunk road but behind a line of trees at GR 668 737. Follow this in turn until it takes a sharp left turn and you can slip right to follow the blue 'Route 5' cycleway through the hedge and onto a wide pavement right beside the carriageway.

Follow this safe but slightly disconcerting route for about 500m until it dives back into the hedgerow to emerge on the outside of a sharp bend on a quiet lane; bear right into the village of Abergwyngregyn or Aber as it tends to be known. In the village take a left turn just after the dilapidated buildings, again following the blue 'Route 5' sign, but not for long. Take the narrow road right, between houses, signposted 'Rhaeadr, Falls, 1 mile'. Point 1.

The road eventually crosses the river at a humpback bridge and most traffic will bear right into the Aber Falls carpark; you however must carry on as the road kicks up steep and climbs out of the valley and into the next one to the east. Continue to the small parking area right at the end of the road, go through the gate and out onto the open hillside at the 'No vehicles except for access' sign, GR 676 716.

Head north up the rough track for a few hundred metres until you pass under the first line of horrible pylons that march over the hillside. As the track bends to the right keep your eye open for a track heading off to the right over the grass; take this. Point 2. The track gets more defined as it begins to climb the side of Foel Dduarth and dives into the hidden

valley around the corner. Climb steadily with some respite and plenty of clear swimming pools below until steeper sections lead you right up to the dam wall at Llyn Anafon.

Note, this track is actually a public footpath over CROW land but the National Trust for Wales have been pragmatic in granting cyclists access provided they "respect the rights of other users and ride in a sensible manner". The track is used by heavy plant from time to time so please respect any temporary closure signs. They also request that cyclists do not ride the similar track up onto the summit of Drum to the east as the whole area is subject to a comprehensive conservation management agreement.

Retrace your steps until you are once again under the dreaded pylons, this time turn right following their march to the east until after a couple of steep rocky climbs you reach a crossroads and signpost. Point 3. South lies the restricted route to Drum and north the grassy bridleway home so turn left at GR 693 722 and head towards the sea. Follow the main track to the left and then when you emerge through a wall onto an open grassy hillside bear left again down the side of the long straight wall. This is a fast grassy descent but beware of the many mountain ponies and suicidal sheep which will inevitably bolt if you scare them. Wind down to a surprise, sting in the tail just after a gate to reach a minor road above the village GR 682 738.

Turn right for a few hundred metres then left down the 'single track road' which zig zags into the back of the village. Left at the T junction then right at the next one next to the Llanfair Arms, this leads you back to the crossroads and traffic lights from the beginning of the ride, cross these and descend to the beach and carpark.

Clwydian - Somewhere in the Clwydians

INTRODUCTION - Sunday Ride.

Sunday 24th May '09 - Today I was up bright an early for me so that I could pick up James in Dwygyfylchi for 8.30 and then meet up with Lloyd at the bottom of the Clwydians for a Sunday ride. The promise was for glorious weather and we were all keen to make the most of it.

If your over-riding image of North Wales is Snowdonia then the Clwydian are like another world. Gone are the steep craggy slopes to be replaced with rounded heathery hills. Out are the rocky tracks and racing rivers, in are grassy trails and bubbling brooks. Steep valleys have morphed into wide open spaces and it feels more like Herefordshire than Wales with high quality arable land and dairy herds.

The hills run NW to SE with the highest hills at the northern end. We were starting at the top and working our way down. Only one snag, to get to the top we needed to start with the biggest climb of the day, a real steep, straight out of the blocks, grunt of a climb. We could have driven up but that would have meant finishing with it late in the day, not a good plan.

So the first 20 minutes of the day turned out to be the hardest. Once up on the spine of the wide backed hills the views opened out with glorious sweeping tracks of fertile farmland leading towards the high mountains of the west. To the east the Cheshire plain and on to Liverpool, to the north the frantic waving of semaphore from the off shore wind-farms spelling who knows what, and to the south, well just what is that mountain, and that one and...

The day developed into a 44km weaving journey, first one side of the mountains, then the other. Climb, descend, climb, descend, climb... Grassy tracks laced with sheep shite grenades spitting up from the rear tyre of the bike in front. Wooded paths winding dappled up and down the valley sides. Long gentle climbs followed by some flowing and entertaining fully powered up descents.

It is a great time of the year to be out in the countryside, all the trees are in blossom and a glance across a valley lets you know the make and model of each tree, Apple, Rowan, Sweet Chestnut, Hawthorn, Cherry, Blackthorn and more. The warm air was full of wafted scents, bluebell, gorse, broom and wildflowers unknown. A friendly buzzard let us get within a few feet before hopping three fence posts down and repeating the process several times.

This was not a racetrack ride but a green lane exploration of pastures new, still hard physical toil but mixed in with nature's natural highs. The sun got stronger and stronger forcing us to look for shade when we needed to eat or rest, or when James had to fix the chain that he had ripped apart.

The offroad ended after a long forest climb lead to a fast descent to the civilization of the car park butty wagon. Tea, burgers, sausage sandwiches and the biggest heaviest chunk of cake in the history of Sunday rides. Later, satiated, we set off on 15km of undulating back lanes to get us home. Playing chicken with steep blind bends, craning our necks to see around sweeping corners,

ignoring the pubs with lubricated clientele sitting out under parasols and sweating the last few steep tarmac climbs each of which lead to the reciprocal rolling racing rollicking downhill dash.

Karma repaired.

ROUTE 06 - Clwydian North

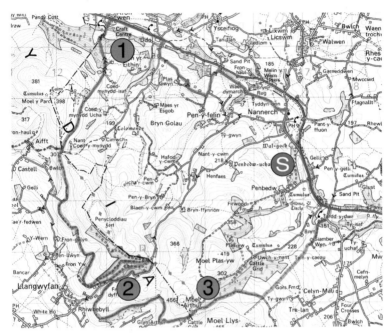

Gradient profile

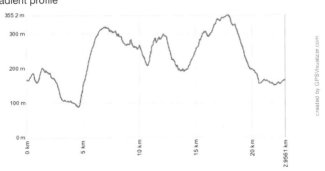

ROUTE 06 DETAILS - Clwydian North

Length:	23km
Height gain:	600m
Difficulty:	Red/Blue
Commitment:	2
Stars:	★
Map:	OL 264

ROUTE SUMMARY

This is an enjoyable ride that stays high on the mountain for most of the ride with great views. I have bunched most of the road section together at the start to get it out of the way but you could start at Afon Wen to finish with the road bits.... Most of the riding is straightforward but the byway descent at the end of the ride gives a little more technical riding. The climb out of Afon Wen is a bit of a trial by fire but after that life is good. For those requiring a longer and more physical day combine this route with Clwyds South for an excellent round of the Clwydians that eliminates some of the road sections.

Start from Nannerch, GR 167 695, roll north through the village before turning left at the Cross Foxes pub. Follow the lane up then steeply down to Pont y Felin where a second steep climb then leads to a T junction, go left then immediately round to the right onto a straight. This in turn leads to a fast but **very narrow and blind descent** to a further T junction, right turn dropping down to the A451. Turn left, bunch up and do a fast 1km to Afon Wen, this should take less than two minutes and the visibility is very good on this section of A road.

As you approach Afon Wen turn left towards the Craft and Antique Centre, going from the biggest chain-ring to the smallest to climb the very steep, unrelenting hill for just under 2km. Point 1. Go straight onto the track where the road bends right (private) to the huge antennae; follow the track to an area of junctions. Take the straight on option through a gate (Bridleway sign) and onto a now grassy track.

This leads along the hillside in a fine position for several kilometres and several more gates until a pleasant and fast downhill section brings you to a gate. 50m before the gate (!) a narrower track leads up and to the left where is passes through a small gate into a forestry plantation. This is the track for you, climb pleasantly up through the trees for a kilometre to reach a gate beyond which is a small carpark. Keeping a very sharp eye out for walkers and horses, ignore the gate, turn sharp right and head down, very much back on yourself along the track. When you hit the next track go straight over onto the very narrow and windy singletrack through the low trees; this is the bridleway. Work this enjoyable section before coming back out onto the wide track, and descending to the gate at the bottom of the forest. You have just taken 2km to do what you could have done in 300m, but it was worth it. Point 2.

Turn left onto the road, then first right following the first bridleway sign, do not be tempted by the second one a few metres further on; it does not exist in any organised way. Ride pleasantly along passing behind the makings of someone's fantasy home and then work the leafy track with more effort than expected until you come out onto the minor road leading to Moel Arthur.

Turn left and, watching out for 'silent but deadly' roadies coming the other way, climb to the col. Point 3. On the far side of the col is a plantation. Turn right in front of this down the gated byway, up and along leads down to a speedy descent or two but keep your eye out for the 'Byway, Cilffordd' sign on the left after about a kilometre and a half. Rougher and rutted riding down this byway brings you past a farm and out onto tarmac again after a further km and a half. At the T junction at the bottom of the hill turn left to quickly regain the A451. Turn left onto this and blast downhill once more for about a kilometre to the Nannerch turning, make a left and find your car.

ROUTE 07 - Clwydian South

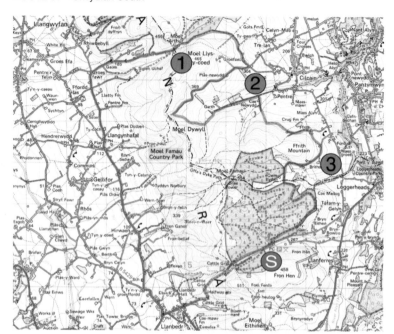

Gradient profile

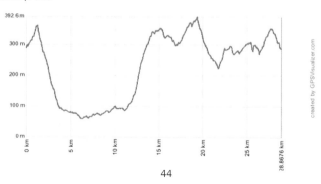

ROUTE 07 DETAILS - Clwydian South

Length:	29km
Height gain:	659m
Difficulty:	Red
Commitment:	2
Stars:	★ ★
Map:	OL 265

ROUTE SUMMARY

Slightly longer and more difficult than its northern neighbour this route gives some excellent riding high on the shoulders of the mountains. The Clwyds North and South combo is the best way to ride these hills but if you are worried about doing it all in one go then the splits give good rides on their own merits. Joining the routes together also removes some of the road sections.

Start from the Moel Famau carpark GR 170 611, turn right out of the carpark and climb up to Bwlch Pen Barra. Drop quickly down the tarmac on the far side until it is possible to turn first right down an incorrectly signposted 'Unsuitable for motor vehicles' lane among the trees. At the bottom of this

carefully join the A494 rightwards for about 100m before turning right again following the B5429 sign. Follow this for about a kilometre then take the first right towards Hirwaen.

Roadie yourself along this road through various villages ignoring any turnings until Groes-fawr GR 126 651 where you turn right and begin the long climb up to Moel Arthur. You finally top out at the Moel Arthur carpark, at the far end of the col is a plantation, turn right down the gated byway in front of this. Point 1.

Follow this track with some nice flowing riding until you reach a metalled crossroads where you should turn right heading up a long but easy climb towards Moel Dywyll. At the end of the rocky part of the track, a little way before the ridge, a bridleway sign can be seen on the left indicating the route down to the little reservoir below. Take this narrow bridleway passing to the south of the lake. Beware of walkers on this section especially towards the bottom where the visibility is less good.

Join a track through a small gate just after a steep bank then bear right along the improving surface. This leads downhill straight as you like and brisk, keep an eye out for bridleway signs on your left pointing to a track on your right, take this. Point 2. Climb hard, ignoring a right turn, out onto the open hillside before reaching a gate as the angle eases.

The track now narrows and contours around the hillside under the trees, first crossing some boardwalk and later a muddy section before a white painted gate leads you past a house. Follow the route downhill, keep going past some farm buildings on the left and through a number of gates. The OS map shows a junction but the route on the ground is continuous and leads finally to a T junction with a minor road. Point 3.

Turn right up the road which soon becomes a track leading up then round and down after a very short, very steep rise. Nice countryside leads into the forestry commission plantation under Moel Famau, turn left climbing a while to a flowing descent and the last long climb of the day up through the forest. No junctions for a while just keep on trucking to the crest of the hill then straight on down a fast track which leads, straight on at a sharp left hander, back into the carpark, job done. The butty wagon here is good value if it happens to be resident.

Berwyn (Llangollen, Corwen & Llandrillo)

INTRODUCTION - Hard Ride, Llangollen Area.

Friday 3rd July '09 - It was raining when I woke up at 645 this morning as Aila got up for work and it was still raining when I got out of bed at 730, Aila long gone by now. Through the window I could see huge joyful stair rods of rain, heavy arrows of water knocking the petals off the roses and replenishing my rainwater barrels. Having had no rain for a couple of months 'thank you' said the garden.

The forecast was for the day to improve as time wore on and so with no sense of urgency I set off for Corwen and my planned big ride. 'Better to travel in hope' they say and as I had gone to the trouble of sorting the kids for after school playing I was definitely hoping.

Later as I changed in the back of the van the rain was still playing timpani on the roof, but it always sounds worse on the inside…

A short while later I was making the climb to the Wayfarer Memorial for the second time in three days, but this time I got to descend the far side of the Berwyn. As I dropped down the long, long, rocky trail I could feel the sky brightening behind me as I went. No swimming today but I did spy a couple of perfect spots for future reference.

Llanarmon Dyffryn Ceiriog is a lovely little village, the pub and hotel both looked welcoming but I had other temptations in mind, more trails beckoned. The climb out of the village is one of those where your brain says 'yes it is that one, and yes it is that steep, and yes there is more around that corner!' Beyond the climb though the byway was a dream, a long easy climb followed by entertaining undulations on a smooth but eroded double track and then a loose descent with a sting in its tail.

Wet slate can be slippery and when it is angled both downwards and across it is doubly so. I was just thinking 'bloody hell that's a steep slab' when the inevitable happened, the back end went and the front wheel went through 180 degrees leaving us both all over the floor in a heap. I say 'we' as my bike and I are becoming a proper team again, joined at the balls of the feet, the balls of the hands and, well, yes, there too.

A km on road and then the final climb, another short sharp shock, leading to more pleasant riding on the open hillside and now in bright sunshine under a blue sky. I hit a road when expecting a more rudimentary byway and for a minute was tempted to just whizz down in the sun. Fortunately common sense prevailed and I hunted down my Plan B for that section instead.

A corker it was too! The fastest descending of the day on a narrow grassy trail through the thistles and then just as fast with bracken closing in on both sides, no margin for error... I got the sense that this was not ridden very much, if at all, a hidden gem and very much worth the effort of finding it.

Onto a rough cutting into some woods now and suddenly, out of the blue, my fist proper crash in a long time. An instantaneous, high speed, over the handlebars still clipped in to the bike wipeout, followed by a roll with the bike flying above and around me to end up in a tangled mess. I was now an cyborg, half man, half machine, bits of metal sticking painfully into places where bits of metal oughtn't be.

Over the last 2km to the road I had to backtrack a couple of times to find the right line, once I knew where it was it all fell into place and what for a minute or two looked confusing and complex became logical and pleasant.

Closing the loop for the day involved 6km of Dee valley back roads, another pleasant surprise. This was not the valley I knew from countless high-speed trips along the A5, this was a very quiet, almost traffic free stroll through what felt like parkland. I even saw a farmer cutting thistles with a scythe, not the kind found on the back of a tractor but the Grim Reaper variety. "Whether you're a king or a little street sweeper, sooner or later, you'll dance with the Reaper!" All in all a 5 star day.

ROUTE 08 - Berwyn & Bronwen

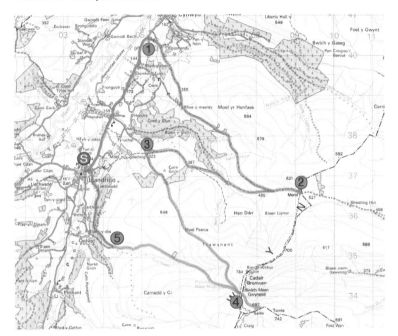

Gradient profile

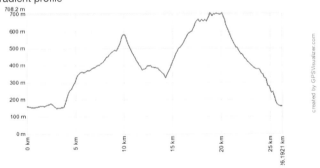

ROUTE 08 DETAILS - Berwyn and Bronwen

Length:	26km
Height gain:	1000m
Difficulty:	Blue or Red
Commitment:	4
Stars:	★ ★
Map:	OL / Explorer 255

ROUTE SUMMARY

This 'double top' route starts from the carpark and conveniences in the village of Llandrillo GR 035 371, on the B4401 to the south west of Corwen. 4km of road work leads to 22km of off-road with two long climbs taken on track and grass respectively. Remote and wild feeling, especially in the second half, this route gives wide views and interesting cycling with some technical interest. Shortening the route to just the first half of the ride reduces the grade from Red to Blue / Red though there is still 500m of climbing to be undertaken.

Start from the carpark. Turn left following the road for approximately four km until it is possible to turn right on a dead end minor road which leads directly through a farmyard at GR 052 404. Point 1. Follow this road very steeply to its end continuing along the track through fields until it meets another minor road. Turn left along this as it very quickly becomes a track, first at an easy angle and then slowly more and more steeply as it takes to the open hillside. Another track comes in from below to join you at GR 083 366 and then you struggle up the steep and rocky track to the bwlch or col at GR 091365. Here is the memorial to 'Wayfarer' who died near this spot, still exploring, at the age of 80 in 1956. Point 2.

Back down the way you just came as far as the first track junction, this time take the lower track, descending to reach Pont Rhyd-yr-hydd at GR 072 368 va. Here there is another memorial on a slate bench overlooking an excellent bathing spot should the weather be conducive 'Maureen Stone, a woman of grace, love and laughter'. The track continues with good views and enjoyable riding until reaching a multiple track junction at GR 051 375, just after passing a small wood on the right. If you have had enough then go straight on to Llandrillo in just under 2km. If you still have the desire and energy for the tougher second half of the ride then make a left up the grassy track beside the wall. Point 3.

The track is good but steep until it comes to a field near a recently felled forest, then it gets a little vague for a few hundred metres. Cross the open field in the same general direction on a vague track to the far end of the field where you find both a gate and a better track. Climb this in entertaining fashion just to the south of the summit of Moel Pearce then follow the line of the fence as far as a short flat section at GR 069 351. Here you need to leave the fence line and bear slightly to the right where it crosses some whiteish stones. The narrow trail

then contours around the back of a cwm, reminiscent of a section of the Pont Scethin route, before struggling up to Bwlch Maen Gwynedd at GR 076 341. The reason for the struggle is clearly the work of illegal off-road motor cyclists, and is very frustrating. Point 4.

You can cycle over to the next col beyond the gate but must then return to this point to descend. Drop back down the way you came for 100m then continue along the 'straight down the fall line' path picking your way through the ruts made by the motor cyclists. Later the track does improve and offers some very nice, fast and grassy sections to reach the small wood at GR 058 350. Pass below the wood then cross to the obvious gate, drop down the track a short way before climbing back up to the height of the gate again. A vague and narrow trail now leads across the hillside, through the bog and then gently down to the obvious trail a few hundred yards away to the west. Whatever happens just keep heading towards this track taking as much care as possible to minimise your impact.

Reach the good track with gratitude at GR 049 352 following it to a gate and stile, where you have options. Point 5. The fastest route home is through the gate, then follow the track, the best route is right through the next gate some 20m beyond. Go through the second gate (as above) following the grassy bridleway along the edge of a field until it is possible to join a forest track at another gate. Take the lower track into the forest and enjoy the descent as far as a wooden gate at the bottom edge of the trees. Just beyond this gate a vague track breaks off to the right and continues under the eaves of the trees, take this at GR 038 364, if you reach a leftward hairpin then you messed up and need to go back 100m.

The track under the trees leads you along and down to a house, metalled road and then after 2 left turns, the carpark is on your right.

Tempting Bending, Berwyn & Bronwen

ROUTE 09 - Llandrillo & Llangynnog

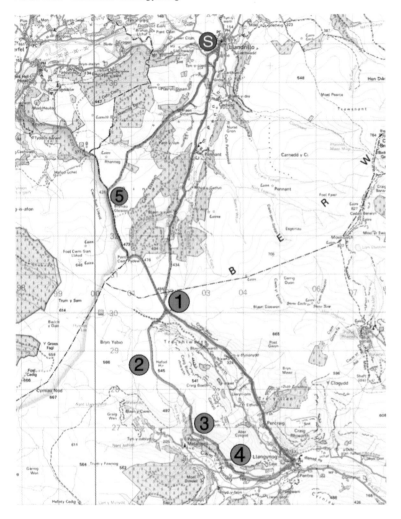

Gradient profile

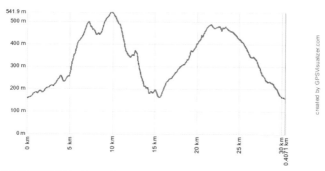

ROUTE 09 DETAILS - Llandrillo and Llangynnog

Length:	30km
Height gain:	1000m
Difficulty:	Black or Blue depending on route
Commitment:	4 or 1 depending on route
Stars:	★
Map:	OL / Explorer 255

ROUTE SUMMARY

This difficult route starts from the carpark and conveniences in the village of Llandrillo, GR 035 371,on the B4401 to the south west of Corwen. You should be prepared to navigate some tricky ground and also to carry your bike for about a kilometre through the heather. This is not a route for the inexperienced but if you are up to it then it is well worth the effort for a day exploring where others fear to tread. The same kind of route as Ysbyty Ifan and Trawsfynnydd, you have been warned! It is however only the middle section that is tricky so if you fancy a pleasant

and easy ride then just do the two
sections between Llandrillo and the
B4391, starting with the northern
section.

Start from the carpark; take the bridge
over the river heading into town, take
the first left and then make sure to bear
left at the fork 100m beyond. Follow
this narrow country lane up Cwm
Pennant to take a right fork at a phone
box above Pennant itself. Keep to this
road as it heads towards the steep back
wall of the cwm, ending at Blaen Cwm
farm.

Follow the track between farm
buildings, through a gate then over
a ford to a steep and rough climb
below the trees. This goes on for a bit
so apply yourself and make sure to
take the obligatory rest at the gate, go
straight over the cross-tracks to enjoy
an open and easier-angled section to
reach the road at GR 018 302.

At the road bear left and then after
about 200m double back on yourself
to the right on a track below the road;
now the fun begins. Point 1. Follow
the track as it bends back to the left
making sure not to take the footpath

off to the right as you head around
the top of the cwm but instead bear
left down a grassy trail after the stream
and opposite a small copse of trees. Go
through a gate then cross a footbridge
(with another ruined bridge upstream)
onto the open moor beyond.

From here you need to strike up the
hillside heading more or less due
south. Find that electronic compass
on your gps and follow it; do not be
tempted to follow the stream to your
left. If you look on Google Earth you
will see that there have been many
peat cuttings on this moor and that
the route is bisected by several. If you
are lucky you will prove that it does
still exist, particularly on the second
half of this leg. At some point (about
a kilometre from the bridge) you will
reach a fence line running east west;
hopefully you will be able to see the
gate in the fence marked by some tall
fire beaters, GR 016 285. Point 2.

Go through the gate bearing slightly
left and crossing over to a second gate
a short way off. Through this gate to
follow the fence line for some way
heading south east, the best riding is
just to the right of the trail which is cut

with a narrow and annoying rut. As the fence bears away to the left (east) the trail does so too but at a distance. You can see the forest that you are heading for in the middle distance but need to stay high for a while yet to get there. Play hunt the trail for a little heading east then when you find the good trail it leaves no doubt; jump on, turn towards the south and enjoy the descent to the top corner of the forest, GR 025 273.

The trail keeps to the top edge of the trees through a gate then after a few hundred metres it steps out from under the eaves of the trees at a gate with fields on the left and woods on the right, GR 026 269. Point 3. Don't be tempted to go through the gate and down, too easy; go left along and just above the wall. In the high bracken season this is 'interesting' and the best technique when the foliage gets too thick is to get the bike on its back wheel, pushing it in front of you to clear the way. The trail does exist however and a lot of fun is to be had by blasting hard through the fronds until the inevitable happens and you find yourself lost in a sea of green after a reasonably innocuous wipe-out.

Once again you can see the top corner of the woods ahead but slightly above you so leave the wall to make a short climb and then contour over to the forest corner, GR 032 266. Follow the good trail along the top edge of the woods to a new gate and then descend quickly until you go through two gates and come out at a couple of houses on a track. Point 4. You soon join a private road so bear left along this for about 300m before jumping off it again down a short steep bridleway cutting back to the right. Cross the grassy field to reach a public road, go left again and make easy work to Llangynog.

So that's the tricky bit done and you may be glad of the hostelry in the village for a minute or two before beginning the long climb back up Cwm Rhiwarth. Turn left at the junction and climb the B4391 all the way back up the valley to the north west; the views are good though and you can spy out the route of another bridleway that crosses the hill you just traversed and works its way back up the valley floor, another day?

You top out more or less where you crossed this road on the way in, keep going along the flat and then down towards Bala some 15km away. You go around the back of a gully before descending a long straight road. Take the second track off to the right, not the forestry one but the byway at GR 003 331. Point 5. This turns out to be a rough track, semi-paved which leads down all the way to Llandrillo some 5km away. Turn right at the junction, cross the bridge and find your car.

The road goes ever on and on, down from the door where it began... Berwyn & Bronwen

ROUTE 10 - Llangollen

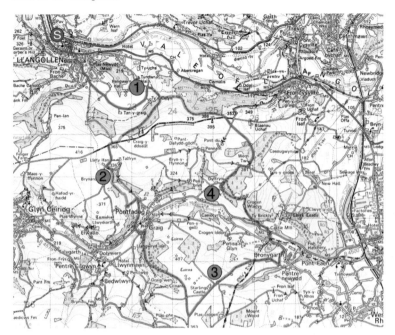

Gradient profile

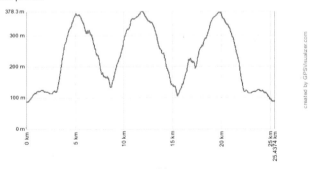

ROUTE 10 DETAILS - Llangollen

Length:	25.5km
Height gain:	900m
Difficulty:	Red
Commitment:	3
Stars:	★ ★
Map:	OL / Explorer 255

ROUTE SUMMARY

An interesting ramble around the hills directly to the south of Llangollen on varied surfaces. Three big climbs, three long descents and a fistful of fine views including Chirk Castle and Offa's Dyke. Start from any one of the carparks in Llangollen where all the usual amenities are available.

Make your way to the traffic lights in the middle of town then turn towards Shrewsbury, or east along the A5. Immediately on your right is an area of right turns, take the second one just after the small traffic island and then go immediately left up a narrower road between houses and following the Plas Newydd sign. This road quickly leaves the town behind and strolls through the picturesque Pengwern Vale; the hillside on your right looks ominously steep, does it not?

At the far end of the vale the road makes a sharp left turn (back to Llangollen) and it is possible to turn right up a loose track, GR 233 411. Point 1. Climb sickeningly up this hill for as far as your resources will allow before taking a right fork onto a slightly easier-angled track along the wood side. More steepness leads into the wood and then after a gate the angle slowly eases as you pop out onto the hillside in a fine position above the valley. There is a paraglider take off here about and so you may have aerial company as you climb the long track over the shoulder of the hill.

The track meets the road at the very top of the hill; turn right then second left to begin a descent into the Ceiriog Valley. You need to take the first sharp left on the way down and then keep a very sharp eye out for a well hidden track on your right after about 100m or so on the apex of a left-hand bend, GR 224 391. Point 2.

Drop onto the track immediately crossing a small stream before following the trail behind some pheasant breeding compounds. The trail then gets steep, rocky and loose having first been grassy and rutted; later it gets overgrown and vague for a short while (stay above the hedge line) before popping out onto a minor road near a farm. Head down the hill away from the farm to a right turn leading to another farm. At this turn right in front of a barn (opposite the kennels) before taking the obvious left fork onto the narrow byway. Enjoy this until you reach a lane; continue on left to reach the B4500 at GR 230 377.

Go straight over, up the lane then first left at a house before climbing away into the woods. At a crossroads make a sharp right to begin a long 2km climb.

The road slowly becomes a track as it steepens before you come out into high farmland and reach a cross-roads. Go straight over then left at the minor road which you follow along then down to where the road goes right, but the byway goes straight on at GR 251 364. Point 3.

The byway quickly steepens and roughens giving an excellent bit of descending between high hedges. Stop when you see the interpretation board. This is Offa's Dyke and over the style to the left is a fine view of Chirk Castle. Continue down the byway until it reaches a road but rather than joining the road you take a left turn down the rough byway for more fun that brings you out onto a narrow road. Turn left and then next right on a very steep road which quickly leads to the B4500 again, beware! Go straight over the road and onto the narrow lane opposite at GR 263 377.

Time to start the last long climb; this one rambles a bit more gently than the last two. Follow the lane until it brings you out at some white houses, bear right and climb more steeply until you pass a house gaining rougher ground with added steepness. The route winds round the back of a small valley before entering some woods. At the cross-tracks take the left and downward option which brings you onto another minor road at a house. Go right (straight on) to climb up to another road, go sharp right then quickly around the back of a house on the improving but steep lane. Point 4.

After a bit of a fight you bear right on a better road then drop to a left turn onto an even better one, GR 258 392. This leads you up and over the top of the hill, back into the Vale of Llangollen. As you begin to get views back into the valley a road comes in from the right and a signpost shows Glyn Ceiriog and Froncysyllte in opposite directions. At this point go straight on, through a gate and onto a track which will take you all the way down into Pengwern Vale. It is steep, loose and fast; beware walkers and horse riders but enjoy the descent, particularly the bit you climbed up so steeply at the beginning of the trip. At the road turn left to roll gently back through the vale and down into Llangollen.

Chirk Castle

ROUTE 11 - Tregeiriog

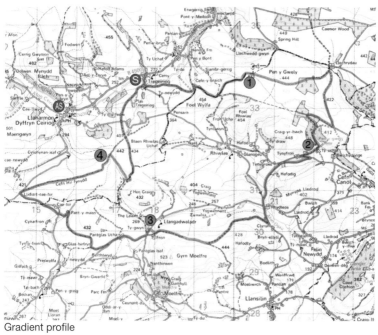

Gradient profile

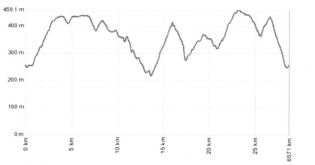

created by GPSVisualizer.com

ROUTE 11 DETAILS - Tregeiriog

Length:	27km
Height gain:	950m
Difficulty:	Red
Commitment:	4
Stars:	★ ★ ★
Map:	OL / Explorer 255

ROUTE SUMMARY

An excellent ride on varied surfaces, grass, track, rock and rut with a relatively small proportion of very minor road. It feels somewhat longer than 27km due to the nature of the riding surfaces which mean that plenty of time is spent climbing but also out of the saddle. There are a couple of long climbs but several more short ones to sap the legs. The final descent is excellent but will drain tired legs and arms. Great views and some adventure with potential for extending the route to the south or shortening it to the west.

Start in Tregeiriog; there is organised parking in the area behind the bus shelter and phone box in the centre of the tiny hamlet. Alternatively (and probably more sensibly) Llanarmon Dyffryn Ceiriog is only 2km further up the valley and has more facilities and space.

From the parking at Tregeiliog turn downhill and roll to and over the river Ceiriog bridge. On the far bank is a crossroads; turn left along the leafy lane heading east to reach a farm after about 1km. Follow the track beneath the farm and out into the open fields with a climb to a gate. Turn right uphill to reach a left turn at a road triangle, climb up and away from another farm, through a gate and out onto the open hillside. Take a left turn at a fork in the track then follow the byway through large open fields until you reach a gate at GR 204 338. Next to the gate are two signposts. Follow the bridleway sign along the right hand edge of the next field while the route you have been following goes straight across the same field. Point 1.

Grassy riding leads along the spine of the hillside until you reach the edge of a forest. Follow the left edge of the wood (not through the middle as shown on the OS) before dropping down towards a farm. Before you cross a stream to reach the farm make a right turn through a gate (the lower of the two and marked with route buttons). Follow this trail south, up and over the hillside to reach a cross-tracks at GR 225 325 just after (most of the time) a large puddle.

Turn right along the rough track as it leads you above the forest and sharp cut valley below; follow the main trail and soon you reach a T junction of tracks where you turn sharp left and descend quickly into the valley. You reach the Pen-y-gwely reservoir after some 500m and pedal pleasantly along its south western flank before climbing up above the dam wall. The track turns sharp right but you need to be sharper still as the bridleway

sneaks away from inside the apex of the track's turn by climbing back on itself. Point 2. There is an excellent picnic / view point part way up the climb (flat area on the right) and then the trail continues along above the farm. Reach a cross-tracks to go left, descending quickly into a small wood before reaching a gate immediately after which it is possible to double back on yourself through another gate to descend to the road.

Time for a quick whiz down narrow lanes; turn right then first left dropping through the valley bottom to climb steeply up the far side. After some 400m or so of up take the right turn at the bridleway sign GR 209 301 and settle in to a low gear for a 2km climb taken mostly on grass. The trail climbs up the flanks of the hillside in a fine open position until it reaches its high point with a junction on a sharp left turn. Take the straight on option through a gate now descending the grassy track until a route diversion appears at a barbed wire topped gate signed 'private', GR 181 300. Go through the gate on the right then very steeply down the grassy hillside through two fields to reach a minor road. Point 3.

Climb back up the road to take the first road on the right (not the byway) following this around the hillside to take a right turn onto an obvious byway a few hundred metres after Pantglas Uchaf farm. This leads you through secret ways to a junction of byways where you turn right continuing through the back woods to reach a farm after a further kilometre. At the farm turn left passing below the farmhouse and onto a lane, left and up to a road to turn right and climb. A bit of a fight ensues as the climb goes on a bit then the road does a 90 degree right and immediately after you take a track on the right towards some phone masts.

Climb past the masts before undulating gently along the rutted, grassy track with wide views for some time. Drop down a rougher and deeply rutted section to reach a gate at a col; strangely the byway becomes a footpath here about, so time for some sneaky diversionary tactics. Point 4. Turn right in front of the gate descending a vague path until it completely bugs out at a small copse

of willow. Somewhere in the corner of the copse you can cross the fence to climb up the hillside on your left to relocate the bridleway 20m up. Follow it now above the gorge, through the bracken to pass through a good gate and shortly after meet a track, GR 173 312, easy!

Turn left up the track which is a rough slate slab, nice in the dry, working your way up and over the top of the hill to reach and cross the original byway which is still a footpath. Now it is time for payback, down the rough track to the road, straight over, more rough track, more fun, until you regain a road. Down the road to a cross-roads, left and over the bridge to a short climb back to the start.

ROUTE 12 - Wayfarer's Route

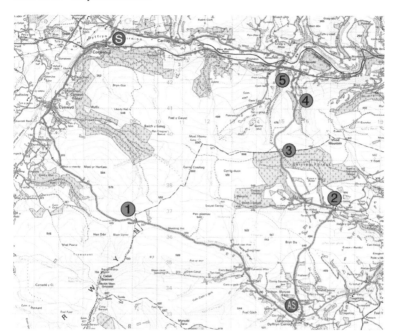

Gradient profile

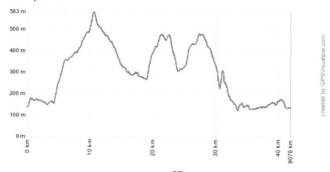

ROUTE 12 DETAILS - Wayfarer's Route

Length:	41km
Height gain:	1300m
Difficulty:	Red
Commitment:	4
Stars:	★ ★ ★
Map:	OL / Explorer 255

ROUTE SUMMARY

This long and enjoyable route starts from the carpark and conveniences in the town of Corwen on the A5, GR 079 435. The middle 30km gives some of the most excellent exploring to be done on a mountain bike, wild and remote but never threatening, an absolute classic.

Start from the carpark, turn left up to the main road at the Owain Glyndwr statue then right and immediately left in front of the bank. Take the narrow road between the houses as it leads quickly to the B4401 Llandrillo road; turn left. Pedal through the hamlet of Cynwyd and some 500m after leaving the village take a left turn up a signposted bridleway opposite a house called Tanyffordd. Climb steeply around the back of another house to reach a minor road at a gate; turn left.

Follow this road very steeply to its end and then continue along the track through fields until it meets another minor road. Turn left as this road very quickly becomes a track itself, first at an easy angle and then slowly more and more steep as it takes to the open hillside. Another track comes in from below to join you at GR 083 366 and then you struggle up the steep and rocky track to the bwlch or col at GR 091 365. Here is the memorial to 'Wayfarer' who died near this spot, still exploring, at the age of 80 in 1956. Point 1.

Descend the far side of Pen Bwlch

68

Llandrillo along the rocky and loose track for several kilometres until it becomes a road at GR 129 355; follow the road to Llanarmon Dyffryn Ceiriog. Turn left in the village, cross the bridge and then grit your teeth to climb the minor road straight ahead. Meet another minor road next to a house and take the straight-on option along the track. Follow the main track along the edge of the wood and then across the moors for about 5km ending with a steep and loose descent with sloping slabs of slate across the trail, very slippery when wet. Meet a lane, continue down then up to a phonebox at a junction. Point 2.

Turn left, cruising along the tarmac for about 1km until you spy a house called Fron Heulog on your right, GR 159 373. Just beyond the house take the unmarked bridleway steeply up through the trees and then out across a wide-open field. From the gate next to the wood in the corner of the first field follow the bridleway arrow, crossing the next field to the opposite corner along a vague trail, GR 151 386.

Through the gate into the cleared forest area, turn right at the first junction to follow the main track up to a barrier and just beyond is a junction where you turn left to quickly leave the forest on a minor road. Point 3. The easy and quick option is to follow this road down to Glyndyfrdwy in a little over 3km and about five minutes. For those with energy and desire there is a more interesting and challenging line to the right.

Pick up the top of the bridleway on your right at GR 147 395, it is unmarked but obvious. Follow this wide track down through the heather until you reach a small level area where 4 x 4's come to play. On the right of this area are the remains of a fence and gateway; go through this to follow the fun, fast, grassy singletrack around the hillside and down towards the woods. The trail through the bracken is reasonably obvious as it passes through another ruined gateway and then drops onto a better track running along the top of the wood. Follow the track as it dives into the trees at a gate then beyond the gate it reaches a better track where you turn left. Point 4.

A little concentration will help on the next section. At this point you need to keep an eye out for a grassy track leading down to the right and following the bottom edge of the forest. Take this through a gate and then back out onto a better track just above Tyn-y-Graig farmhouse. Do not drop to the farm; instead continue through a dilapidated gate onto a grassy track running along the top edge of a field. Climb briefly then a short way after carefully crossing the remains of a stile you can drop to the right down a steep track which leads to a field. From above you can see the line of the bridleway, first crossing the field and then bearing left along the old hedge line above a steeper section of ground. Follow this around the back of a semi derelict house (Ty'n-llwyn) and then over to a footpath gate that can easily be seen on the far side of the field. Cross this field directly to the next set of dilapidated buildings, go right between the buildings to join the steep road at a gate with footpath arrows on it, GR 155 421. Point 5.

Descend to a junction, turn left then continue down to meet the main A5 just outside Glyndyfrdwy, make a left turn (using the layby to your advantage) and quickly arrive at the 30 limit. Near the bottom of the dip turn right onto a small road signposted 'Rhewl', follow this over the railway then over the river Dee on a high bridge. Go left after the bridge to enjoy the pleasant scenery and quiet lanes to Carog. Bear right at the junction, continuing through the village and on to a junction just outside Corwen (next to the Leisure centre) where a left turn leads you back to the town carpark.

Mignant & Moelwyn (Betws y Coed & Trawsfynnydd)

INTRODUCTION - Ashley's Ride.

Friday 12th June '09 - The morning after the evening before saw me heading once again down the A470 to Dolgellau, this time to meet up with Ashley Charlwood of Canoe Wales. No canoes or kayaks today just an exploration of some byways and bridleways, prospecting for a route around Rhobell Fawr an isolated 705m mountain to the north of Dolgellau.

After a quick coffee and a gawp at the view of Cader Idris from Ash's front window we set off to Llanfachreth a couple of miles away and the start point for the ride. Life is so much easier when accompanied by a local guide (as Martin said of me yesterday) and even if, as today, he hadn't ridden every yard of the route before, he knew where every section started and finished which made navigation that much easier.

The beginning was a pleasant amble along lanes and grassy bridleways with high and clear views back to Cader Idris brooding in the near distance. Then a bit more road before a long gentle climb on a remote mountain track to the east of Rhobell Fawr. Time to catch up on the news, swap views on whatever and soak-in the pleasure of being out on the hills.

Through a high forest for a while before breaking left into the trees on a vague track. Ash wondered how long he would stay on his bike and the answer was about 100m, then he did the first of two excellent face plants, most entertaining and gave me plenty of warning of where not to go.

The trail soon came out into a clear felled area and that is where the trouble began. At first we could identify the route of the bridleway by the different plant growth along its length, bog cotton and wild flowers. Later the forestry operations had obliterated the route as surely as if it had suffered the blitz. Carrying the bikes and jumping drainage ditches lead us to where we guessed it must dive back into the trees but the clearing of the mature trees had allowed the wind to completely devastate the new forest edge.

I left Ash and the bikes to plunge hopefully into the darkness and, lucky me, I soon found the route about 40m away. Snapping as many branches as possible we forged our way to the bridleway and continued down the Tolkienesque Mirkwood way, prospecting is great fun and sometimes gives up nuggets like this. Then there was a scary 'Night of the Living Dead' cabin deep in the trees, we didn't go in.

Back out onto the moor and the second of Ash's up and overs, I managed to ride straight by to some rude utterance or other "Jammy B'stard!". We soon regained the obvious and started the back loop, once again on the tarmac.

Ash pointed the entry point for kayaking the Mawddach and I suggested that you would have to get out for Rhaeadr Mawddach waterfall some miles below. Not so! Some mad crazy fool has made the drop, mental. I remember cramponing over the falls on an amazing ice arch one night during the winter of '85, mental…

The ford was cooling but the climb up to Bwlch Goriwared was not and I could feel my legs begging for a day off, Ash was just powering away. Then I realised that I had ridden for 12 of the last 16 days and as Phil pointed out yesterday evening, I should probably be faster if I were not so worn out! Time for a few days rest, weather permitting.

After a chat with some fellow bikers at the col all that was left was a hop, skip and a jump back down the far side to the van. Now if I can just get the Forestry Commission to waymark that 300m section and send in a man with a chainsaw for a couple of hours…

ROUTE 13 - East of Betws

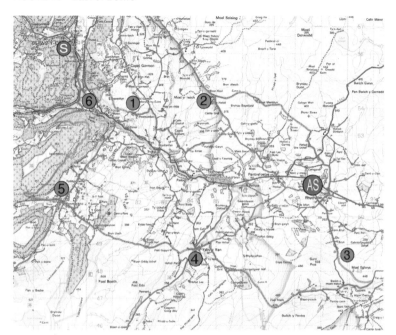

Gradient profile

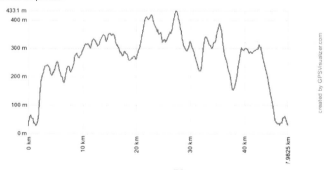

ROUTE 13 DETAILS - East of Betws

Length:	50km
Height gain:	1500m
Difficulty:	Red
Commitment:	3
Stars:	★ ★
Map:	OL / Explorer 17 & 18

ROUTE SUMMARY

This is a long and involved ride linking remote bridleways and byways with sections of equally remote mountain road. The route uses quiet and rarely used tracks to join communities together via a series of climbs over mountains and moors. If undertaken in the wet then the ride will feel a lot longer given the nature of some of the riding and there is little shelter except for the final few kilometres. An inauspicious start leads to a long and satisfying day for those who enjoy exploring. Start from anywhere in Betws y Coed (or Dolwyddelan, or Ysbyty Ifan) and look forward to a bit of pretty much everything!

Start by taking the minor road that passes behind Rock Bottom outdoor equipment shop in Betws y Coed, GR 795 561. Follow that road south until you reach the A470 where you turn left, cross the bridge and turn immediately right on the track after the bridge. Follow this bridleway for 100m or so passing in front of a property until you see a gate and footpath sign on your left; take this. Climb up to the A5 crossing this directly to a break in the wall on the opposite side.

Continue climbing (pushing) up the steep zig-zag path up the hillside, probably wondering what this would be like to descend, until you emerge onto a forest track. Turn right to reach a lane, bear left and climb up the hill until at the top (just as Cefn Rhyd comes into view) you reach an area with a number of junctions. Take the right turn leading into the trees up a track beside a stone building. Follow this to the aerial compound and the locked gate blocking the track. Cross this carefully then follow the track as it winds around the open hillside with good views back into the mountains. Keep to this track, ignoring any left turnings, until you reach a metalled road near a gate GR, 815 538. Point 1.

Turn left at the road as it leads you through a number of farms before a short climb and descent to a better lane. Turn right onto a fast descent before bearing first left (there is a farm road that appears like a road just before) down and then steeply up again. A brief respite on the flat is followed by a short descent then the road bears round to the left at a junction, GR 838 523. Go through the farmyard as the road kicks up once again then out onto the open moors to reach the B5113 at Pen yr Orsedd. Go left here as a short climb brings surprising views of the high peaks (weather permitting) as you re-enter the National Park.

Just over a click on this road leads to a right turn on the outside of a fast

bend. Point 2. Climb up the dead end minor road and onto the Pentrefoelas moors as the road slowly deteriorates to become a grassy track at GR 864 544. Go straight on along the track, as the road goes right to a farm, heading into the boonies, fighting the mud and dodging the sheep. When you reach a cross tracks, go straight over keeping to your present track until at GR 885 531 on the brow of a hill you see the wall step away from the track briefly and there is a gate on the right (if you descend to a gate then you are 100m too far). Go through the gate on the right and that track soon improves as it leads down to Hafod-y-Dre-Uchaf farm.

At the farm bear left descending to the A543 where a short left right shimmy disposes of that road and you follow instead the minor lane round then down to the A5. Beware the A5 which you meet quickly just after a humpback bridge, cross it directly and carefully into the tiny village of Rhydlydan (pub). The road bears right into the village before you take the first left turn heading south west. After 500m on this road go left at the crossroads where two of the other roads show as dead ends. This road gives a long straight climb so get your head down until you see a bridleway sign on your left at a gate, GR 896 475. Point 3.

Onto the good track, still climbing around the hillside taking a left fork where offered and slowly finding the going getting harder as the surface deteriorates, finally becoming grassy on the brow of the hill before descending to a road. Go right here and free of all the sucking grass make a pleasant road descent heading generally west. After three km of easy going you pass through a gate near Blaen-y-cwm farm and the road climbs up once more onto the shoulder of Foel Frech and the col, at Bwlch Blaen-y-cwm, GR 872 476. At the col the road finally gives up to become a muddy track, much more entertaining!

Just keep heading down the track with one good ford until you reach Cerrigellgwm-isaf farm which you go straight through and onto a road. Climb again for half a kilometre to bear right at the junction and begin the descent to Ysbyty Ifan. After a quick 1.5km go left at the T junction to continue down into the village. Cross

the river to a T junction, go left and then almost immediately right up a narrow lane just before some houses. Point 4. Gird your loins for another stiff climb as the road gets steep and then where it goes right to a farm you go straight on up the technical and steep byway; ride if you can.

Luckily it does not go on like that for too long and you soon emerge gratefully onto a minor road. Go right up the last little climb before following the road around to the west. After about a kilometre and a half it too gives up the ghost to become a good track at GR 818 490. This long but not too steep climb carries you over Bryn Llech and down to Penmachno via an enjoyable but sometimes washed out descent. Hit the road above the village to finish the descent on the tar as it brings you out at the bridge in the middle of the village. Go over the bridge to be faced with The Eagle Pub, which does food. Where the road goes left in front of the pub you go straight on onto the narrow lane. Point 5.

Leaving the village is easy enough to start with but once you have made sure to go right at the fork then things steepen up in the trees. Keep climbing hard until you spot the Penmachno MTB trail crossing the road, GR 776 508, (signs for drivers to beware bikes and horses); time for something completely different. Go right following the red trail signs for the next five kilometres enjoying the well designed singletrack of 'Loop 2' until you emerge onto a forest road just after some climbing zigzags at GR 794 534. The trail sign number is 225 and a footpath crosses the track at the same point to make identification easier. The trail goes left but you go right to begin a long fast descent off the mountain,

but beware horses!! At the fork bear right and then when you hit the next wide track go sharp right continuing downhill at a pace until you reach a road after a quick 2km, GR 798 539. Point 6.

Almost home, at the road go left dropping down to a bridge that leads to the A470; cross this to a stony cyclepath on the far shore, bearing right along this following it to it's end. Here you go left retracing your steps along the back road to Betws y Coed which you reach after a little more than a kilometre.

Fantastic views and fine riding leading back down to civilization in Penmachno, a finish along Loop 2 beckons but still needs to be earned. East of Betws

ROUTE 14 - Ysbyty Ifan

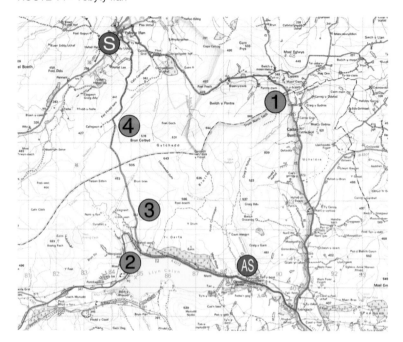

Gradient profile

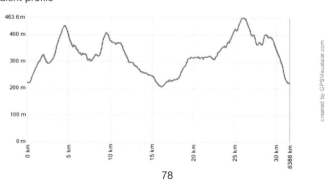

ROUTE 14 DETAILS - Ysbyty Ifan

Length:	32km
Height gain:	750m
Difficulty:	Red
Commitment:	4
Stars:	★
Map:	OL / Explorer 18

ROUTE SUMMARY

This is a tough and sometimes very vague little route requiring good navigational skills on the return leg and the ability to maintain a good sense of humour in adversity. Do not attempt this route unless you really, really want to and have the skills and equipment to look after yourself. In the unlikely event of spotting other riders on the return section it is probably best to avoid them and hide. They may have been lost on the moors for days and cannibalism is a real possibility, unless of course it is you that has been lost for days.

Start from the small carpark in the village of Ysbyty Ifan, GR 842 488, just over the bridge and on the right next to the playing fields. Toilets are a little further along the road and up a side street.

Head out of the village along the road next to the carpark climbing immediately and soon steeply to a right turn onto a narrow road on the right after some 500m or so. Follow this lane heading into the hills until it is possible to turn first left down a metalled road heading down to Cerrigellgwm Isaf farm. Go through the farmyard to take the obvious gate on the right that leads to a ford (and foot bridge) then onto the start of the byway heading south east.

Follow this (entirely rideable) up to Bwlch Blaen-y-cwm then through the gate onto the semi-metalled track beyond. Zoom down this as the track becomes a road at GR 881 472. About 1½km later take the first real road on the right (signposted Bala) just as the road begins to climb. This leads around the hillside and then shortly after a gate with a Celtic knot-work post you go straight on along a wet track where the road goes sharp left. Point 1.

This disgusting trail leads somehow along, up and over a cross-track then out onto a minor road at a wood. For once it is a relief to get off the off-road. Bear right and enjoy the scenery as you undulate along to meet the B4501 at GR 912 426. Bear right again and make short work of the quick road to reach a T junction with the A4212. Work your way gently up to Canolfan Tryweryn, the national white water centre at GR 892 401. Here the riverside café offers refreshments with a view of the kayaking, rafting and general water-based mayhem available. Make the most of the civilization on offer as pretty soon it will all feel like part of another lifetime.

Back on the A road continue climbing up to and along the edge of Llyn Celyn to reach a point at GR 850 412 where the road is bending right. You can just see the Memorial Chapel ahead and a tiny bit of tarmac and road paint is spotted on the right, hidden in the trees. Point 2. Take this lonely looking byway which quickly improves after a tired gate. Sadly you soon leave this behind by taking a right turn alongside a wall and over a stile. The track beyond is hard work for a while but improves, luring you up to and past some farm buildings in about 500m. Continue following the rough track above the walls, across the open hillside and away from civilization. At GR 849 423 the main track turns north east and you need to take a narrow trail north west, through a stream and up the wet hillside beyond. Now the trouble begins in earnest. Point 3.

The trail is starting to disappear and your next target is the fence line running perpendicular to the route. The crossing point should be about 100m uphill of the wall on your left. There is no gate or stile but some Samaritan has cut the barbed wire to make crossing safe. From there you need to keep about 100m above the wall, crossing the hillside to reach a rusty old gate through another fence at

GR 846 429. From this point the route is closer to northerly, making its way diagonally across the slope and heading towards the back of the shallow valley that you are in. As you cross the slope, no doubt wondering where the trail went, you will spot a fence with a quad-bike trail close to it on the far side of the valley; this is your target. Cross just upstream of the corner of the fence then follow the quad-bike trail which is sometimes rideable as it takes you up and over the shoulder of the hill to reach another rusty gate before disappearing.

Now it gets proper interesting. Continue in your present direction, crossing diagonally down-slope through tall grass, rushes and bogs. You will reach a stream cut into the hillside which you cross then follow for a while around the left side of a flatter area. Once below this feature strike back under it and continue in that line until finally, after much pushing, carrying and even some riding, you can see some sheepfolds below you and a grassy track appears, saved! Point 4.

Drop gratefully down to the sheepfolds at GR 840 456 before following the

track past them and up a short way to a large wall. Turn right under the wall and make easier time along the good but rough track as it climbs up and over the shoulder of the next hill before dropping down past some houses to reach a road at GR 847 481. This quickly leads to Ysbyty Ifan where a left turn gets you back to the carpark.

ROUTE 15 - Trawsfynnydd

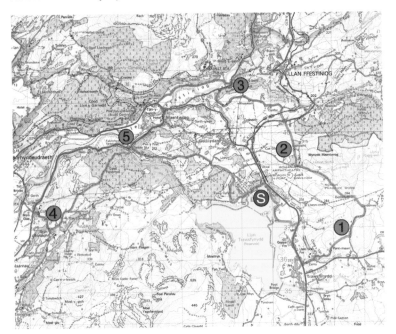

Gradient profile

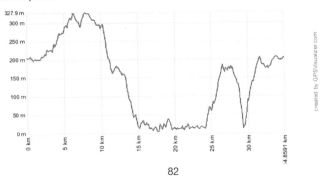

ROUTE 15 DETAILS - Trawsfynnydd

Length:	35km
Height gain:	800m
Difficulty:	Red
Commitment:	2
Stars:	★
Map:	OL 18

ROUTE SUMMARY

Every guide needs an esoteric ramble through bridleways lost and found with variable riding and tricky navigation, hide and seek on a bike. This route provides such entertainment for those who enjoy something different and complex. Not a ride to do unless you are competent with a map and happy to make do with rough and at times frustrating riding. On the other hand, some of the riding is blissful!

Start from the visitor carpark at Trawsfynnydd Nuclear Power Station (disused), GR 696 383, left out of the carpark and then almost immediately right towards some boarded-up buildings. Around the back of the buildings follow the 'Route 8' signs

which you then proceed to follow through the woods near the edge of the lake etc until you come out on the main A470 at GR 706 365.

Turn right making the most of the cycleway beside the road until you reach the second junction into the village of Trawsfynnydd. Turn left up the steep and walled road opposite, pass the cemetery and then when the road goes right you go left in front of a terrace. Ride the lane around the side of the houses, past the kids' playground and then follow the bridleway sign along the back of the houses. This track leads you past a couple of farm buildings and into the countryside. Just keep to the main track (ignoring a left turn to some buildings at GR 719 363) as it crosses fields and becomes progressively more grassy. Just after a gate on the brow of a hill you will need to bear slightly right as the track becomes a path and runs to the right of a fence, heading over to some buildings a short distance away. Point 1.

Go between the buildings at GR 725 367 and then onto a good track heading off in roughly the same direction (north), climbing gently around the hillside. The track then descends with good views into the hills and now you must look out for a track heading off to the left just before the track does a sweeping turn to the right. There are two entries to this track; take the second one and then go more or less direct to the wall about 100m away ignoring better tracks that climb up and over the small bluffs to your left. At the wall you should find an old stile with a yellow marked post. Cross here and then push your way over the wet ground and rushes heading towards the pylons.

You should aim to pass to the right of the pylon by about 25 – 40 metres and from there head over to the gate and footpath marker in the wall; not much riding in this section but it is

quite short. The gate leads you on to a narrow path and, while this is not quite in the position (wrong side of the wall) as marked on the map, given that you have been signed this way it makes sense to follow it to the left. Drop roughly down to the edge of the picturesque ruined farm and sheep pens, GR 726 389, then follow the good track around to the left. Take the second, easier angled, right fork up the brow of the hillside and then follow this grassy track to Braich-ddu quarries (no longer used). Straight through the quarries and out along the good track beyond which leads to a minor road at GR 708 389. Turn left and almost immediately (at a cattle grid) lift over a stile (footpath sign) on the right to join the bridleway which is marked with painted arrows. This quickly brings you out onto a track and, even though this may not be quite the line of the bridleway, follow the track that you have been signed onto as it leads you to a farm. Point 2.

Around the back of the farm is another footpath signpost leading to the grassy edge of a large field, climb up this along a well restored slate fence to reach another stile and signposts. From here it gets vague again. Strike across the field heading down but not towards the gate and stile above a ruin as the line of the bridleway is through the gate some 50m to the right. Take a vague line more or less straight down-slope from here until it is possible to curve around to a lonely looking signpost in the middle of some rushes at GR 704 402. From there go straight down a short distance to a signpost and stile above the road.

Dog leg over the road and back along a fence to a stile into an open field; cross this then descend a fenced track which leads under the nuclear railway and out next to Cynfal-fawr farm. Follow signs around the right hand-side of this then the track to the minor road at GR 703 407. At the road turn left to enjoy interesting views and an excellent, long, swooping descent to reach the A496. Turn right along the road for about 300m before making a left turn just after a bridge perched high above the Afon Cynfal. Point 3. Make sure to go left again immediately back on yourself along a minor road that winds its way along the valley to emerge at the A487, GR 662 409. Turn left and make the most of the

cycleway beside the road leading into the village of Maentwrog. From here it is an A road section for the next 6km until you arrive at the village of Llandecwyn, GR 621 375. Luckily the road is not too busy and has good visibility for most of its length. Make a left turn opposite the toll bridge turning to pass through the hamlet and then climb steeply up the hillside for a kilometre. After a short sharp climb you will arrive at a junction next to a phonebox. Go left here and freewheel to the picturesque Llyn Tecwyn Isaf. Point 4.

From the lake make a left and climb up steeply again to the end of the road next to a small chapel where there are excellent views down to the Dwyryd estuary, Portmeirion and back into the high mountains to the north. Take what is now a track up and over to Llyn Tecwyn Uchaf where it follows the northern edge of the lake along a narrow trail through low gorse bushes perched high above the water. Climb away from the lake and drop into the forest beyond turning left once in the trees. Through the trees make sure to bear right at a fork and then keep your eyes open for a narrow track dropping left off the main trail just after you pass through a wall.

Descend in entertaining fashion to reach a gate where you go left and drop down to the A496 once again close to Maentwrog Power Station, GR 653 395. Go past the station entrance before taking the first lane on the right leading to a long wooded climb up the Ceunant valley. Point 5. You pass over the water pipes that supply the hydro scheme before going through a second forest; a short while later the road makes a sharp left turn but you follow the Route 8 signs off to the right. This is now a pleasant trail through the trees to a sudden meeting with the nuclear plant. Keep following the signs with a wary eye for slightly dodgy positioning as you ride around the back of the station (big isn't it?), pass a lakeside viewpoint and finally ride along the barrage above the lake to reach the carpark from whence you came.

Long, long grassy climb to sap the legs.

ROUTE 16 - Rhoberll Fawr

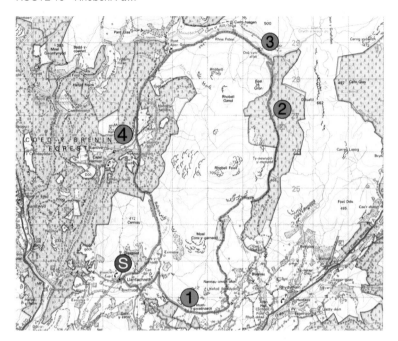

Gradient profile

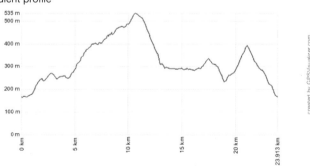

ROUTE 16 DETAILS - Rhoberll Fawr

Length:	24km
Height gain:	600m
Difficulty:	Red
Commitment:	3
Stars:	★ ★
Map:	OL 18

ROUTE SUMMARY

An entertaining ride on high mountain tracks with a dose of adventure thrown in for good measure. Wide views, intimate navigation and a feeling of remoteness complete the atmosphere on this ride. Start from the carpark just east of the school in the picturesque village of Llanfachreth near Dolgellau, GR 756 225. There are conveniences a few yards away towards the village and all the facilities of both Dolgellau and Coed y Brenin are but a short drive away.

Note, a short section of this ride covers ground that the Highways Dept in Dolgellau believe to be public highway as do the Forestry Commission, the landowner is unsure though they do presently tolerate access. Given all this I have presumed for access and included the route. However, should things change and signage to that end appear on the route then please respect that information. The section is the short track from the farmhouse to the road just after Point 3.

Leave the carpark turning left (east) to roll along the tarmac for about a kilometre before turning first left up a minor road (gate) at GR 761 221. Climb pleasantly along this road until at an obvious sharp bend a track leads off to the right heading towards a house some 100m or so away. Take the track but where it bends left you go straight on through a gate and into the field beyond, through this and continue across the next one in the same direction. For the next kilometre the theme is 'keep going along the wall' and despite this being a bridleway you will encounter more stiles than gates so the chances of horses are slim at best. Keep following the obvious route above the forest and take the right hand (lower) stile at the end of this descending to a house and minor road at GR 774 216. Point 1.

Turn left along the road for about a kilometre as it continues the bridleway's route around the hillside. After a few gates the road takes a turn steeply down and right, just before this at GR 786 218 take a left turn heading uphill and due north; it is the first left turn that does not lead directly to a farm. The road gets steeper becoming a track leading into the moorland below Rhobell Fawr. After a couple of kilometres it passes through a small forest on the mountain's southern flanks. Out on the far side of the forest the track gets rougher and the scenery wilder with great views as it works it's way east through a small mine-working before joining a larger forest at GR 797 249.

Turn left into the forest on a smoother track leading upwards for a couple of clicks through the trees. As the trail begins to drop gently and the trees on the right are cleared away it is time to keep a very sharp eye out for a vague unmarked trail leading off to the left at GR 799 269. Point 2. If you find yourself gathering speed and bearing to the right then you are too far....

Drop off the forest track onto the grassy trail on the left and then after about 100m you will suddenly come out into a cleared area. Continue along with the edge of the forest on your left until that too gives way and you face a large open expanse of cleared devastation with little sign of a bridleway. From the corner of the trees bear slightly left traversing an area which the different vegetation tells you was a forest ride and heading towards the rightmost small copse of trees on a high point of land. Cross a small stream and climb up to the trees riding (surprisingly) most of the way. At the copse it gets worse; from the edge of the copse bear right across the Somme-like terrain keeping the little stream a little way off on your right. The bridleway should re-enter the forest about 20 – 30m left of the stream but (unless it has been cleared as requested) then the edge of the forest is a maze of windblown trees. Find a way through the first few metres and the bridleway miraculously re-appears as a dark tunnel through the trees, the easiest way in is about 50m left of where it should be but everything can change after a good storm. Not to worry too much though as the whole of this vague section is about 500m.

Follow the trail through the forest passing a 'Night of the Evil Dead' shack part way through to emerge into the light again at a small footbridge, GR 798 278. Bear right along the grassy singletrack with the stream below you to the right until it leads you away from the edge of the forest, getting vaguer before dropping on to a small flat area. When you hit this it is time to bear back to the right again as the route does a zig down the hillside, pick up a better trail that zags back along the face of the slope and ends up at a small ruined farm on the valley floor, GR 794 287. Point 3.

Go through the farm then continue on your way along the good track under the hillside and you will soon meet a minor road. Bear left to follow this easily around the hillside with views of the Rhynnog mountain range to the west. Stay on this road keeping left at the junction on the edge of the forest, continuing along, enjoying the smooth ride as the road steepens allowing a fast, flowing descent which is a pleasant feeling after the slow progress a while back. Look out for and take the first turning on the left, GR 759 264 leading back into the forest. Point 4. Keep going straight on at all junctions as the road becomes a track; enjoy the ford, deeper than expected but rideable with speed, or cop out to take the footbridge.

After going straight over the second wide forest road the trail kicks up steeply as it leaves the woods and rejoins the moors heading towards Bwlch Goriwared. The surface is loose gravel at times making for hard work but the climb is relatively short and the col soon arrives. Dance your way down the far side at speed until just before a gate it is possible to take a reasonably obvious track that breaks off to the right, GR 766 235. Speed along this enjoyably until you can bear right through a gate and into a wood at, GR 762 229, watch out for big branches at head height. Drop pleasantly through the wood to emerge at a road / track; cross this but then follow it to enter a fenced track leading through a gate or two down to Llanfachreth. The track emerges behind the school; turn left at the road and the carpark is just a few metres away.

Ash Charlwood drifting through daisies on the Rhoberll Fawr route

Åsa & Matt Strickland with Jim Camis enjoying the view of Yr Aran & Llyn Gwynant from the Siabod Circuit.

Moel Siabod (Dolwyddelan & Capel Curig)

INTRODUCTION - Farewell to Ev.

"Life is like a box of chocolates Forest, you never know what you are gonna get."

It has been a good week, I have ridden four days and got a lot of work done towards the guide. My bike and I are getting to know each other again and the legs are remembering just what the MTB lark is all about. It had been fun revisiting routes that I have not done for a while and seeing just how much has changed in some places.

I had been looking forward to having some company on a ride this Sunday, time to get some photos and see if I am getting fit again or not.

Then on Saturday night I got a call from a flying mate with some bad news. It transpires that Ev (Evan) Roberts who I have known and flown with for more than 10 years crashed his glider into the sea where he lived in Bulgaria and drowned. (I just caught myself and had to change 'lives' to 'lived', such is the perception transition of someone moving into the past tense)

He learnt to fly at the same time as me and we shared some of that intoxicating first flying experiences camaraderie. He was a local bloke from Anglesey and we frequently nattered in Welsh at takeoff or in the landing field. He was one of those cheerful types, always pleased to see you, always a smile and a fairly matter of fact attitude towards setbacks.

Having worked hard on ships for years he had saved his money and bought some land in Bulgaria to speculate with, speculation that seemed to have paid off and he was intending to come home this year. He kept sending me pictures of flying sites (taken from the air) that he was visiting and they always seemed to arrive when the weather here had been crap for weeks, perfect timing. There was usually a cheap pair of trainers poking into the photo, then bare legs, just to rub it in that he was flying in shorts in great weather.

Not so on Friday when he took off in poor conditions and immediately got into trouble, crashing into the sea from 100m up. A friend alerted the emergency services then jumped into the water to try to help, but his body was not recovered for another two hours.

Ev, I hope you went quick mate, I hope you didn't suffer, "Bon voyage" and "Hwyl" from me. Catch you on the flip side.

So today was bitter sweet, an old friend gone and some new ones being made, life goes on until it stops. The riding was great, the sun shone and the crashes were innocuous, funny even. We chatted and joked, admired the views, sweated the carry and worked the climbs. The descents were sweet in the early afternoon warmth and we were only a little bit late back.

In the words of Talk Talk,

"Life's what you make it, Celebrate it, Anticipate it, Yesterday's faded, Nothing can change it, Life's what you make it, Can't escape it.".

ROUTE 17 - Bwlch y Groes

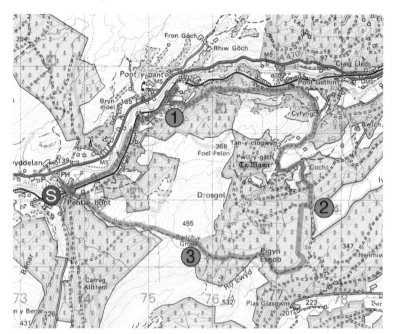

Gradient profile

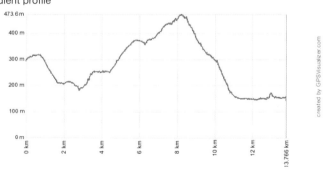

ROUTE 17 DETAILS - Bwlch y Groes

Length:	14km
Height gain:	350m
Difficulty:	Red / Yuk
Commitment:	3
Stars:	*
Map:	OL 18

ROUTE SUMMARY

You can use this short route in a couple of ways, either as a training ride when time is short or as an optional add-on to any of the nearby routes such as Sarn Helen or East of Betws. It is best left to midsummer when the ground has dried out as it can be, and often is, a quagmire. This is in part because of the terrain and partly because it sees a bit of off-road motorcycling traffic which cuts it up bad in places. It is a real mix of forest track, 'natural' singletrack, very minor roads and even has a bit of purpose-built singletrack for good measure. Start from the roadside parking in the village of Dolwyddelan, GR 735 524, where there are the usual amenities and a railway station.

Beware horses in these parts as there are a couple of riding schools nearby.

Start from the junction in the middle of the village of Dolwyddelan following signs to the railway station; turn towards this but keep to the little lane that runs past the carpark. Follow this as it degrades to a rough track following the Afon Lledr downstream then passing under the railway to climb up then descend to a house where it reverts to a minor road. Follow the road past another station until a couple of hundred yards beyond this you can turn back on yourself to the right up a steep and rough track. This leads past a couple of houses and then into the forest. Point 1.

Go left here following the good track

96

along what some locals call 'the golden mile' for about 2km. Keep a sharp eye out for a narrow grassy path making a break to the right and steeply uphill at GR 773 536. This byway gives a short entertaining climb and an even shorter and more entertaining descent before emerging from the forest at an old house called Cyfyng. Turn right at the house negotiating a nasty climb up a steep-sided valley.

Soon you climb into a hidden valley and both the road and angle improve as it snakes up and into the part of the forest used by the Penmachno MTB trails loop. Keep climbing until at GR 775 519 a forest track heads off to the right and you should see Loop 2 emerge from the trees on the other side of the road. Point 2. Take the track on the right now following the signposts for the Penmachno Trail for about 1km. The trail climbs up some open hillside before diving back into the trees; a short rocky section leads to a brief opening that the trail crosses on a slightly raised berm. This opening is the byway and your chosen route lies up it to the right, GR 774 509.

Unless you are here in the driest of dry seasons this byway will be wet for the next 2km. It is also likely that you will end up pushing a fair bit over that distance. Follow the obvious line of the byway, cursing and swearing and falling into bottomless bogs as it leads you through the trees then briefly into the open before diving back in again to reach the col at Bwlch y Groes. Point 3.

The narrow trail now drops to a fence at GR 756 513. Here you go left along the fence to a good gate overlooking the grassy hillside beyond. Drop down that hillside keeping a little way to the right of the fence until you can bear slightly right to go through a gate before crossing back to a good track. The track comes as some relief and gives a pleasant descent all the way to the back of the village. Head to a gate just to the right of a house, through the gate and another just beyond to go left in front of the house. This track soon becomes a road that leads quickly into the village proper and salvation.

ROUTE 18 - Moel Siabod

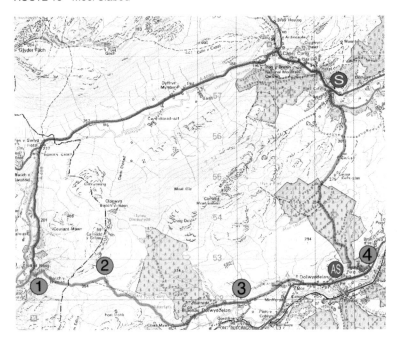

Gradient profile

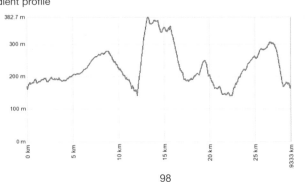

ROUTE 18 DETAILS - Moel Siabod

Length:	28.5km
Height gain:	1200m
Difficulty:	Red
Commitment:	3
Stars:	★ ★
Map:	OL 17 & 18 or Landranger 115

ROUTE SUMMARY

This is an excellent ride if you can see past the initial road bash and following carry. It takes in some high and remote moorland with novel views. The riding is at times challenging and technical both on the flat and descending, good bike skills being essential in order to get the most from this route. There is no shelter on the higher sections of the route and it is definitely best to avoid this route during the wet season unless you are better than competent. Start from the Bryn Glo carpark outside Capel Curig, GR 735 570. Alternate starting points are to be found in Capel Curig (behind Joe Brown's) and at the Forestry Commission carpark a few hundred yards uphill from the Swallow Falls Hotel.

Start by taking a right out of the carpark, following the road into the village then taking the left turn outside Pinnacle Pursuits café and outdoor shop. Follow this wide A road past Llynnau Mumbur all the way to the Pen y Gwryd junction near the hotel.

Either, ignore the junction, carrying straight on down into Nant Gwynant at speed on the winding road. Keep a weather eye open for a couple of gates and a footpath signpost on your left just before a left-hander, GR 657 527. Point 1.

Or, where the organised parking at Pen y Gwryd ends is a gate and stile on the right of the road. The byway beyond offers a slower but off road descent of Nant

Gwynant. Follow the track which becomes a road until it rejoins the A road. Turn left climbing back up a short way to the bridleway. Point 1.

That is the 20 minute road section dealt with; hopefully you will be nicely warmed up by now. The trail now leads steeply up through the trees on an un-ridable path so a carry is the order of the day for the next 600m or so. The views open out as you climb above the trees to reach a gate through a wall, when you decide to ride again depends on your fitness as much as the terrain; from the wall it is all rideable, but hard work. Things slowly ease off and by the time you reach the next gate you will have been riding for some distance with high views of Snowdon behind you.

Go through the gate to descend the grassy path beyond; this is a wild and rough track giving tricky riding on rock, grass and mud. As before, fitness and determination are the keys to success, not to mention a canny eye for the best line as you head over towards a small copse of trees in the middle distance. Just before the trees is a very deep washed-out gully to climb

over before passing above the trees to locate a vague junction leading off to the right. Point 2. This leads down the fairly obvious route just to the east of the trees and heading for the stream.

Cross the stream on a flagstone bridge at GR 678 522, climbing up through a gate and shortly after you reach the head of a better track. Bear left along this with good views of Moel Siabod as it leads you over the shoulder then down towards the Lledr Valley via an excellent bit of loose descending. Reach a farm at the head of a road at GR 693 513; turn left through the farmyard descending the quick road to a junction where you go left again.

This road leads easily along the valley floor until just after a short climb you pass through a farmyard that straddles the road. Point 3. Here you need to bear left as the road goes right, climbing past some farm buildings and sheep gathering areas to leave the farm at a gate. The track soon forks; the right fork is the correct line, leading out across open fields on a reasonable track. As the track begins to drop it gets very rocky and overlooks the stunning Dolwyddelan Castle which you ride right past joining a better made track to continue in the same direction. Drop down at speed but beware walkers as you reach a hairpin with a track leading off from the apex through a gate. Go through the gate and descend to the main road.

At the road bear left to follow it into the little village of Dolwyddelan with its amenities. Carry on through the village soon leaving it behind as you hunt for the way back over the mountains. Point 4. This is located where a forest track meets the road at GR 744 527 (if you pass the old garage then you are just too far);turn left on the potholed track which soon begins its long gentle climb up the flanks of Moel Siabod. Meet another track, turn

left then pass around a forest gate / barrier and continue climbing as the trees slowly give better views.

There is a junction at GR 731 547 after a long straight section. Here you bear right and soon leave the forest on a rutted but smooth track, this is a fast section of gentle climb which at times almost feels like descent. The route leads you over the shoulder of the hill with views back over to the Glyders and Carneddau before it drops steeply down the far side on a rough and loose track, giving an entertaining descent back to a minor road. At the road turn left to follow it to the main road at Pont Cyfyng, turn right carefully onto the main road and descend to the Bryn Glo carpark a few hundred yards further on.

Mixed riding near Bwlch y Rhediad, Siabod Circuit.

ROUTE 19 - Sarn Helen

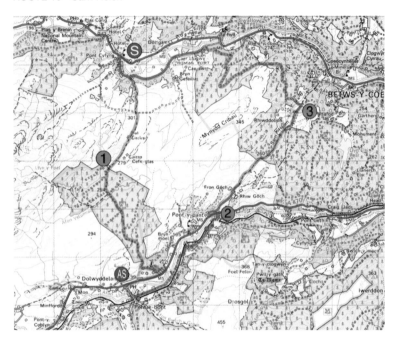

Gradient profile

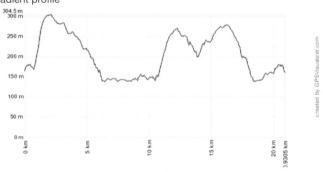

ROUTE 19 DETAILS - Sarn Helen

Length:	20km
Height gain:	550m
Difficulty:	Blue
Commitment:	2
Stars:	★ ★
Map:	OL 17 & 18 or Landranger 115

ROUTE SUMMARY

Easier than its more western sibling around Moel Siabod this is one of the more accessible routes in the guide and one of the most enjoyable, a classic mountain biking journey. The riding is never too technically difficult or testing apart from the first hill, but that will quickly degenerate into a push for most people. The second climb is steep too but this one is rideable if your lungs can cope. Great views, lots of history and some fine riding make this one a must. There is a café at the start / end of the route and others in nearby Capel Curig. Alternate starting points are to be found in Capel Curig (behind Joe Brown's) and at the Forestry Commission carpark a few hundred yards uphill from the Swallow Falls Hotel.

Start from the Bryn Glo carpark outside Capel Curig at GR 735 570. Go out of the car park, turn right and nip along the main A5 as quick as you can to take the first left over Pont Cyfyng. The road leads past a few houses and then down to where it is possible to take the signposted byway off to the right next to the former chapel at GR 736 567. Climb past the chapel, go through a gate and then play 'who can get the furthest' up the steep, loose track, never seen it cleared yet.

The track slowly improves as it climbs over the shoulder and out onto the open hillside with great views back into the high hills behind you. Navigation is easy, just keep straight on along the main track as it heads southwest over the shoulder with some lovely riding, especially in the dry when it gets fast and smooth with the odd jump and chicane to play with.

Point 1. All too soon you will reach the edge of a forest at a gate, GR 731 548, dive straight in to come out at a large junction with a signpost, bear left along the wide track, still descending. Keep to this track all the way through the forest until you reach a forest barrier a short way above Dolwyddelan, where you have a choice. Either go past the barrier, around the hillside and bear right to descend to the road on a good track or, go right before the barrier to follow the rough track which drops very steeply at one point to bring you out between the houses in the village.

Either way once at the road turn right and head into the village with its pub and shops until you reach the village centre. Turn left at the obvious large junction heading to the railway station just over the river bridge. Turn left as if heading to the station but ignore the carpark and keep going along the narrow lane which leads out of the village and along the riverside passing the odd farm on the way. The road gets rougher and rougher until it is a stony

track with a challenging short climb before it drops back down past a house and morphs back into a road once more. Follow this to a junction in front of a large house / hotel, go left, cross the river and reach the main A470, GR 755 539. Point 2.

Turn left and nip quickly along that road to take the first possible right turn after some 200m, take a deep breath and psych for the climb. You are now on the roman road Sarn Helen which climbs steeply up into the Gwydyr forest. Keep straight on at the 'perfectly timed for a rest' gate as the road turns into a track with some interesting climbing challenges. You reach the forest at a level section, dive in through the gate and go straight over the first junction. The track soon starts to descend through the trees with the odd gate to pull you up sharp; keep on down until you meet a wide track at a cross-tracks, GR 773 561. Point 3.

Go left here to quickly reach a three way junction on a hill, break left and continue climbing for a short way before undulating through the forest. After about 700m take the next left at a fork climbing past a forest barrier and then contouring around the hillside. Keep to this good track now for the next 2km until you wind your way down to another forest barrier above a junction. Through the barrier, left and then right descending a quick track, **but beware families out walking.** Take the first available sharp left turn which leads around the hillside to emerge onto a minor road at GR 751 573. Left

along the quiet road with good views of Moel Siabod, pretty soon you will be back at the former chapel climbing back up the road and reaching the main road at a T junction. Go right carefully and scoot quickly back to the carpark.

Moel Siabod from the Sarn Helen route

ROUTE 20 - Betws to Bryn Glo Link

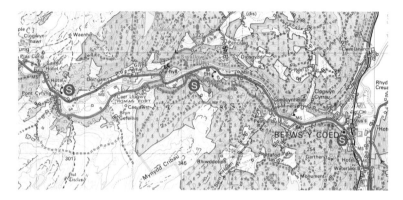

ROUTE SUMMARY

Given that a number of noteworthy rides (Sarn Helen, Circuit of Moel Siabod, Llyn Cowlyd) can start from the Bryn Glo carpark GR 735 571 between Betws y Coed and Capel Curig, and that many people stay in Betws y Coed it is sensible to include the most traffic free route between the two points. Hopefully this will encourage riders to leave the car back at base and treat the link as part of the route or a pleasant warm-up.

Gradient profile.

Ride out of Betws heading towards Capel Curig on the A5 heading west. Just before the 40 mph limit ends and the road goes dual carriageway a little lane heads off to the left. Take this, turning immediately right up a short steep hill between houses. The road quickly becomes a forest track that you follow until it is possible to bear right around a forest barrier just as the track you are following becomes 'Closed to Vehicles'.

Keep to this track now through the trees (a short climbing challenge is to take the obvious rocky track trickily up left for a few metres before bearing right back to the present track) until it brings you behind a compound and you reach a larger track at another barrier. Go left back on yourself and climbing for about 100m before turning first right onto a smaller rougher track. Climb up this for a short way until you drop down and finish steeply as you enter the very top of a forest carpark / family picnic area. **Please ride slowly as a number of family walks lead off from here.** Cross the grass leftwards to the track then descend through the carpark until just before reaching the A5 it is possible to bear left up a straight steep track which leads up, down then gently up to a right hand turn around another barrier. Follow this track around the hillside, go straight over a cross tracks and down to emerge onto a minor road. Left along the minor road until it starts to climb (the Sarn Helen route goes left here and Moel Siabod returns) through some houses to a bridge. Right at the bridge and the Bryn Glo carpark is just a couple of hundred metres along the A5.

BRYN GLO TO BETSW - 8KM

From the carpark turn right along the A5 then first left over Pont Cyfyng and along the minor road beyond. As it drops away from the houses the Sarn Helen ride goes off to the right and Moel Siabod descends the same track. Follow the quiet road for about 2½km until you enter an area of forest and can take the first track forking off to the right into the trees. Climb quickly straight over a cross tracks then climb around the hillside before a more level section leads to a junction at a barrier. Go left here soon climbing then descending steeply to the Forestry Commission carpark / family picnic area. **Please ride slowly as a number of family walks lead off from here.**

A fantastic position to be in, high above the estuary, Cader Idris in front, Bwlch y Rhiwgyr route.

Rhynnogau (Llanbedr & Tal y Bont)

INTRODUCTION - Bones of the Landscape

The Pont Scethin route always takes me back, back to the days when the Rhynnogau were my playground. I played on their lower slopes as a young boy, free to go where ever I chose as long as I was back for dinner. As I got older I spent every summers night during the school holidays bivvying in the heather with a bunch of mates, making fires to cook on, looking at the stars and generally growing up.

Later, in preparation to another year's alpine climbing, I would spend hours on training runs from Barmouth to Diffwys and back along the ancient byways. I had a girlfriend who lived on a farm at the other end and would sometimes walk back from her house over the hills. I even did my first mountain rescue with the then Rhynnog Rescue Team (now South Snowdonia) when we went searching for a suspected suicide that turned out to be a 'Reggie Perrin'.

So you might say that I am well acquainted with this wild and lonely group of mountains. My kind of place, my kind of karma.

Today was my quarterly full body mole search with my skin consultant. I always get a bit wound up before this event, I have that imagination thing going on where the consultant turns to me and says, "Well its worse than we thought Mr Bursnall, looks like we might not have caught it in time after all..."

But happily today was not that day and if there is anything more galvanizing than a positive prognosis then I have yet to find it. Its like a three monthly kick up the arse that reminds me to get out and make the most of things, not that I need much provocation, but sometimes we can all get a little complacent, there's always tomorrow...

On the way home I went prospecting for a new way in to the usual Pont Scethin ride from Tal y Bont. I wanted to add a little more riding and to take in more of the countryside. In the end

I worked a route from The Victoria pub in Llanbedr, climbing steeply up quiet country lanes to join the old coach road high up in the mountains. Excellent.

The weather was kind with both cols opening up for me as I approached cloudbase and a day that started cold and windy ended hot and sunny. The saddest part for me was seeing the amount of selfish destruction wreaked by thoughtless off road motorcyclists, they really do know how to make a mess. I imagine that these routes were in a much poorer condition when they were being regularly used for their original purpose, driving a coach & horses over the hills, but that is not excuse enough.

The mud here is an incredibly slippery variety, within a second or two it can turn your knobbly tires into slicks that spin uselessly, time to get off and push. It also leads sometimes to the impression that your tires have gone flat, I actually had to check once today, just to make sure.

The bones of this old landscape though are hard, several thousand years of human habitation can be seen as you ride around. Burial mounds, forts and hut circles can be located in abundance with just a cursory glance at the map. There are huge clearance mounds in some of the fields and skylarks sing over moorland bordered by some incredible dry-stone walls. This place will outlive us all, this place will survive the scratches and scars of modern transport abuse, this place is welcome to my bones when I have done with them.

110

ROUTE 21 - Pont Scethin

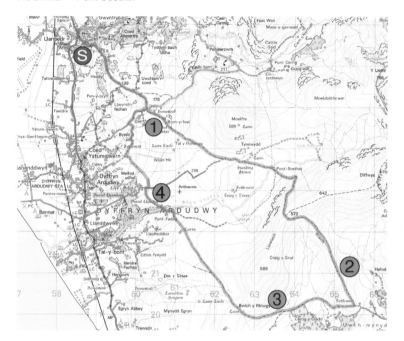

Gradient profile

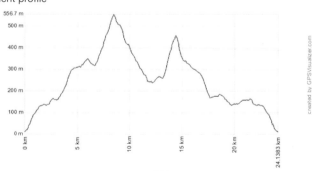

ROUTE 21 DETAILS - Pont Scethin

Length:	25km
Height gain:	900m
Difficulty:	Red
Commitment:	3
Stars:	★ ★
Map:	OL 18

ROUTE SUMMARY

One of my favourite rides, possibly because I used to run much of both it and the next-door Bwlch y Rhiwgyr ride when I was a youth. The riding is good but the views are exceptional, high above the sea with Cader Idris and the Mwddach Estuary making guest appearances. It is one of the oldest inhabited landscapes in Wales and stuffed full of history. It beggars belief that they used to take a coach and horses over the initial climb.

Start from the roadside parking close to The Victoria pub and public toilets, GR 585 268. Drop to the main road then turn left in front of the pub and cross the bridge. Take the next left after the chapel following this road steeply at first out of the village. Keep to this road until you reach a T junction where you go left and then almost immediately right down the dead-end lane leading to Bron y Foel farm, GR 603 249. As the road bends left towards the farm close to a stone outbuilding take the right-hand fork up a track. Point 1.

Follow this track as it becomes progressively steeper, grassier, muddier and more rutted (in that order) taking care to follow the signposts and stay on the obvious route as it zig-zags up a field then heads off onto the mountainside through a gate. Work your way pleasantly around the flanks of Moelfre until you come out at a gate onto the main Llyn Bodlyn track, GR 622 237.

Turn uphill (left) following this well-made track for a few hundred yards until markers and ruts indicate where the packhorse route heads off to the right over the moors towards Pont Scethin. Drop through mud and rocks to reach the bridge then fight your way up the other side on flagstones, grass and rocks until it is possible to get back on your bike again. The views here are tremendous and as you crest the ridge they open up in another direction with wide and wonderful views over to the Mawddach and Cader Idris.

The descent of Braich on the far side is a rare treat of high mountain riding coupled with the views. Watch out for walkers and soak in the atmosphere; there are few places like this. Watch out for the occasional lump with the capacity to launch you into the air before crossing the wall at a gate and stile before continuing down the ridge in fine position. Great riding leads to a fork in the track at a large boulder; take the right hand option and after the mud comes a nice narrow trail between walls with a much ignored 'No Motor Biking' sign. Point 2.

The path suddenly joins another at a small pointed marker stone, GR 655 202. Take the new path almost back the way that you just came, sharp right to work over a short steep climb; if you reach a minor road then you have missed the junction. Follow this improving track high above the Mawddach with views of the estuary and the sea. After a straight section along the edge of a forest you will descend to and pass through a wall to reach a vague junction where the main track breaks left, GR 637 200. Point 3.

Make a quick right left dog-leg on the grass to reach the bottom of a reasonably obvious slate path heading steeply up and across the hillside; climb this with considerable effort to Bwlch y Rhiwgyr. The start of the descent on the other side is very loose and rocky, just about rideable but there is a strong chance of 'dismounting'. Once this section is negotiated life becomes easy again; just follow the pleasant, grassy track through a number of gates until it brings you out at the top of a tarmac road near a gate. Drop down, over the bridge then up again, passing close to a burial chamber. Point 4.

The next bit requires a bit of

concentration. At the T junction (gate, GR 602 230) go right then immediately through a second gate. After less than 100m turn left following the footpath sign along the edge of the field; it is debatable if this first 100m or so is footpath or byway so best walk to the wall corner. When this leads you into the corner of the next field bear left along it's edge joining a walled track part way down the field boundary.

Follow the track as it heads across the next field and along the left edge of the one after to emerge onto a road, GR 597 238. Turn right along the road, cycling pleasantly along bearing right at a fork with a house track and then right again at a T junction on a hill. This leads back to a junction you will recognise so turn left here to whoosh all the way back to the village, well mostly.

Matt on hard packed late spring snow on the Pont Scethin route.

ROUTE 22 - Bwlch y Rhiwgyr

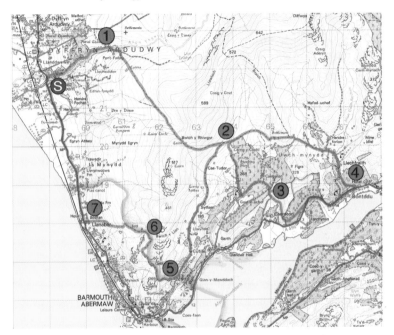

Gradient profile

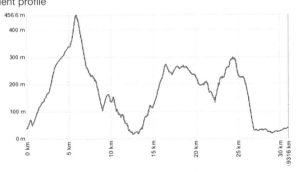

created by GPSVisualizer.com

ROUTE 22 DETAILS - Bwlch y Rhiwgyr

Length:	30km
Height gain:	1000m
Difficulty:	Red
Commitment:	3
Stars:	***
Map:	OL 18

ROUTE SUMMARY

A most excellent companion route to the Pont Scethin ride covering some of the same ground but in the opposite direction giving a very different feel. Basically a figure of eight loop with three steep climbs, amazing views and some great riding on varied surfaces. Easily shortened by about 8km but some good riding would be missed as a result. Start from the small carpark near the bridge in Tal-y-Bont, GR 589 217; there are toilets and a shop nearby. Be warned though, the average angle climb on this ride is 9% and the steepest is 31%, the worst rideable climb in the guide. Because much of this is also on grass this is not a route to underestimate!

Between this route, Pont Scethin, the Mawddach Estuary ride and Cader Loop there are a lot of possibilities for some serious mash ups.

Start from the carpark entrance turning uphill into the housing estate for about 200m until two turnings to the right offer themselves up. Take the second tarmaced one signposted 'No through road' following it straight up the hillside until it becomes a track with a road to a house on the left. Continue up the track with the river below to the right as other tracks and paths meet or cross your path. The climbing gets progressively more technical and challenging, but never un-rideable, until you top out at a road. Point 1.

Go right on the road dropping briefly

to Pont Fadog bridge, built in 1762 according to the stone marker. Back into climb mode once over the bridge as the road bends round to the left and then ends at a gate. Follow the track for 50m until you go straight ahead onto a grassy track beside the wall, fight up the first part of this (if it is wet) until the angle eases and you settle in to a long, gentle, grassy climb. Your target appears ahead and after a number of gates the trail narrows and kicks up steeply for the final few hundred metres, which will inevitably see you pushing or carrying the bike.

The long 450m climb finally ends at Bwlch y Rhiwgyr and the view changes dramatically with Cader Idris and the Mawddach Estuary appearing all of a sudden, well worth a lung easing pause. Drop down the excellent singletrack beyond the col until you reach a track, GR 636 200. Go left but make sure you take the track through the gate towards the forest. After little more than 100m beyond the gate you will take the first track on your right heading down towards the estuary. Point 2.

This muddy trail winds down to the

forest edge and then along it until it reaches the top of a very minor road which you follow in turn. Beware getting too carried away enjoying the sound of humming disk breaks and flowing corners as you need to make the first left turn, GR 641 187. Climb up to the white metal gate then continue along the very narrow lane beyond. This leads past some houses, one of which is home to a fine collection of Landrover 90s, before dropping down through the trees.

After a short climb the road gets steep but again beware going too fast as the bridleway suddenly appears where two gates lead to the same track, GR 650 186. Point 3. The top gate opens but the other is bolted shut, strange. However, the trail beyond is great as it winds around the hillside, hanging high above the estuary with lovely views and good riding, the section through the forest giving some entertainment. Reach the main A496 and you are back at sea level again, all that work, for nothing!

Turn left heading into Bontddu after about a kilometre, climb through the village until it is possible to take a left turn in front of the Bontddu Hall Hotel. Point 4. Settle in for 200m or so of climb over the next 3km, just stick to this road until the climb tops out, GR 656 202, and a bridleway sign points through a footpath gate on the right just as the road bears left. Huff and puff up the next few hundred metres, passing the trail down from the Pont Scethin route on the right.

The narrow trail now undulates for a while in entertaining fashion then runs along the top edge of a forest to bring you back to the gate at GR 636 200, 'Hey, I've been here before!' Point 2. This time keep going straight on along the good track heading south west until after a couple of kilometres you reach the top of a road at Sylfaen farm. Enjoy the road, nice and smooth, nice and quick, especially as it straightens out into a long fast descent, good views too.

Point 5. After a further 2km on the road throw the anchor out the back and take the first available road on the right, just before a parking area. Enjoy the road, nice and steep, nice and slow as it climbs back up the steep side of the mountain. Gaze at the uber steep section ye mighty and despair! 'Go on you can do it' and there is a short rest just ahead before the final nasty steep bit past Barmouth Slabs.

Follow the deteriorating road to its end at Gellffawr, a sometimes empty house, keep to the track as it passes the house then climbs once more but now on sucky grass. The next kilometre is well signed with yellow arrows, basically left at the first junction, right at the second up to the gate and stile. Once more the view changes dramatically as Cardigan Bay arrives in a rush with the Lleyn Peninsula beyond, lovely.

The track wanders about the hillside a bit until it meets the Bwlch y Llan path just after a gate and heads left. Point 6. After a short flat section and another gate the final descent begins with a series of switchbacks then some straight stuff to reach the right edge of a wall. Go through a gate and then left through another with a 'Barmouth' sign painted on the wall, GR 610 180. Head down between the walls, then across an open field with the sea directly below, straight over the track junction and then between the walls once more.

A bit of a curiosity now as the walls come closer and the trail turns into a very steep, fall line descent with rocks as the surface, slippery when wet would be an understatement but great fun if you can cope with it: be prepared to fall off and walk down. Beware loose horses at the bottom of the right of way where you join a minor road to end the descent. Point 7.

At the A496 turn right and make a ten minute mad dash along the cycletrack that masquerades as a pavement until you arrive back in Tal-y-Bont, nice one.

James enjoying the Bwich y Rhiwgyr route.

The author on the scary bit, Bwlch Cwm
LLan, pic Wojciech Zdebski.

Snowdon (Llanberis & Rhyd Ddu)

INTRODUCTION - Double Top.

Thursday night ride time again and this time it was my choice, so no time trials up Elidir and no torture up Snowdon, just a good honest XC ride around the Gwyrfai Valley.

We met at the Rhyd Ddu carpark where I presented Matt with a 4 year old's MTB just in case he had 'forgotten' his bike, again. Five of us, four of the usual suspects and an interloper from 'daan saaf', Martin the time trial man on a single speed MTB and sporting a fine pair of roadies legs.

Another glorious evening and off we set into the big blue taking care not to get run over by the Welsh Highland railway. At the top of the first small climb Åsa had two punctures, the first a thorn and the second a dodgy inner-tube valve. I was quite glad of the rest to be honest as my hurriedly eaten dinner was lying heavy on my gut. Then off to the main business of the first real climb.

The great thing about riding in a pack is the peer group pressure! Someone always rides the bits you might not and vice versa, this provides 'encouragement' and ups everyone's game. Amazing how the first secret of success is to just give it a go, nothing happens if you aren't clipped in and moving the pedals round.

Watching Martin on the single speed was entertaining, his feet seemed to be barely moving at times and yet he was being propelled forwards at a good speed. Too good in fact, out in front and rocking up the steep sections while I was still getting warmed up.

Bwlch Cwm Llan is one of my favorite spots on Snowdon, the wide open and dramatic view never fails to please. We were there just as the deep shadows were crossing the bwlch, a perfect balance of light and shade. As Phil Number 2 pointed out, the air was crystal clear, all the haze of the last few weeks having been blown away.

Descending the ascent is a blast too,

technical and scary in parts with sharp slate knives scattered across the track in jagged piles followed by big culverts and shifting blocks, perfect. Time for the back to become the front as I cleared a few new sections and made it down 100% clean for the first time, so did Phil 2 and Matt, Åsa and Martin were a little more circumspect, they might say sensible. Second secret of success, scope your line on the way up, time spent on reconnaissance is never wasted, as they say in the military.

A short grassy section provided respite after the near multi-bike pileup caused by Matt's tank slapper on the rough track, though I did nearly cycle off a small bluff in my haste for speed. Then into the forest on the far side of the valley.

My anti UV long sleeved top came in extra handy as the midges were out in force and Mr Time Trial was having a trialling time, no stopping, keep the target moving.

Åsa only hopped off the train from London half an hour before the ride and, despite hubby Matt's best attempts to feed and prepare her, she needed a banana stop shortly after Llyn Llywelyn. At the lake the fish were rising all over the place to snatch gnats from the evening air, perhaps this planted a subliminal feeding suggestion in her mind.

It is a long climb up to the top of the forest to a descent only I had done before and I could hear jocular mutters of decent as I took the 'wrong' turn at a fork. Mutiny was afoot but thanks to the fact that I was out front with Martin nothing came of it; no one had to be hung from the yardarm or cast adrift in the ship's boat. I was finally warmed up, enjoying the climb and looking forward to the payback.

We gathered at the top of the descent to admire the view, less than 45 minutes before we had been at a similar altitude on the opposite side of the valley looking back this way. This is one of the things that makes this ride so good, a real sense of journey.

Down through the brash with mud, ruts and that bloody log that gets me every time. Following Martin and Phil at speed down the last bit my front wheel suddenly started surfing the loose surface, I thought I was going to die, time for new tyres.

Out of the forest at last for the final testing section to the pub, deep ruts along the route were the obstacle, they kick you over or spit you out if you catch a pedal and rimming the front wheel on a rut can highside you in an instant, line choice is the key and everyone done good. The final secret of success is... surprise! It is amazing what you can ride if you don't see it coming and have to stay upright to survive.

A pint by the fire in The Cwellyn Arms followed a short midge ridden ride back to the car. Matt spat his out "disgusting things" but I just swallowed them and enjoyed the free protein. What better revenge could be meted out to those tiny 'spoil your whole day' devils?

ROUTE 23 - Bwlch Cwm Llan & Beddgelert Forest

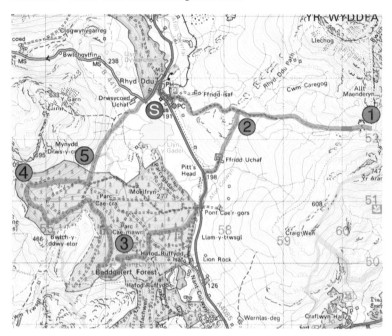

Gradient profile

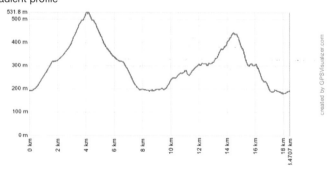

ROUTE 23 DETAILS - Bwlch Cwm Llan and Beddgelert Forest

Length:	18.5km
Height gain:	600m
Difficulty:	Red
Commitment:	2
Stars:	★ ★ ★
Map:	OL 17

ROUTE SUMMARY

A very enjoyable 'double top' route with outstanding views, excellent riding and some tricky challenges; beware of walkers. Start from the Rhyd Ddu carpark at the bottom of the Rhyd Ddu and Llechog routes up Yr Wyddfa, Snowdon, GR 571 525. The Welsh Highland Railway also has a station here. The carpark is pay and display and also has conveniences. There is a good pub in the village.

Start by cycling past the toilets to the far end of the station where a set of gates allows you to cross the railway; the first climb starts here. Follow the wide track away from the railway until you reach a fork; take the right fork passing around a gate / barrier. Climb the wide rocky trail as it snakes its way

upwards with good views to a further gate and stile at the crest of the hillside. On the other side the trail descends slightly heading straight towards the obvious col in the distance. At this point you should note the 'Llechog' path heading off through a gate on your left and the grassy trail weaving away through rushes on your right. That is your descent later.

Chase the trail towards the col, easily at first but harder and harder later; keep to the main track and beware large open quarries at wheel-level to your left. You will end up making a couple of short carries over slate waste sections, the second of which is rideable on the way down if you are brave or foolish enough. At the top of that very steep but short incline the trail crosses a flat quarry area following the fence before dropping onto a flagstone path leading to the col and the wide and wonderful view it offers. Point 1.

Once satiated, retrace your steps (pedals?) taking care on the obvious sections and definitely keeping a good space between you and those quarry holes now close by on your right. Remember that grassy trail through the rushes? It is just after a gate on the first piece of up after leaving the col some 2.5km behind. Turn left onto it. Point 2. On the map it leads straight to Ffridd Isaf farm some way below, in reality it wanders a little around muddy sections, streams and so on before a final very muddy section leads you to the farmyard. Right then left through the farm before tarmac leads to the A4085; turn left along this for half a click then first right at the forest.

The layout of this forest has changed somewhat with the return of the Welsh Highland Railway so take the main track downhill for a short way before crossing the railway at the obvious crossing point. Beyond this follow the track along to bear left at the first

junction and then shortly afterwards right on a narrower slate waste track leading steeply upwards. This soon takes you up to Llyn Llywelyn where you should turn left along the lake's retaining wall. There is a nice picnic spot here should you need a chillout session. Point 3.

Continue along the retaining wall then bear right around the lake until you have almost circumnavigated it and can take the first left up a steep forest road. Follow this up then along until you reach a wide junction in a little dip, keep left, climbing again to a fork where you bear left again climbing some more as the track gets less well used. You soon come out of the woods and work around the back of Cwm Ddu with forest on either side but in an open position. Point 4. Now keep an eye out for a narrow path leading off to the right through the brash, if you reach the end of the track you are a few hundred metres and a fair bit of climbing too far.

Drop onto this trail around the hillside then steeply down with a few surprises, roots, gullies etc on the way until you reach a wider track. Go left, then immediately left, then immediately left again climbing up a narrow rocky path that soon leads out onto the open hillside with great views to the right. Point 5. This narrow and deeply rutted path leads around the back of Cwm Marchnad, it can be frustrating if you choose the wrong line and get rutted but whichever way you go there is a 'get off and carry' section to cross a steep tumbling stream. Continue round and down with more ruts and a few large drop offs until you end up at a gate.

There is a smaller gate on the right; follow this trail around the edge of the field to reach a road, bear right to descend into the village then go right again at the T junction. Pass the pub (fine ales and good food) climbing back to the edge of the village and the carpark, job done.

The author heading up to Bwlch Cwm Llan via the entertaining climb, completely rideable bar 20m, Llyn Cwellyn below. Pic Wojciech Zdebski.

ROUTE 24 - Moel Eilio

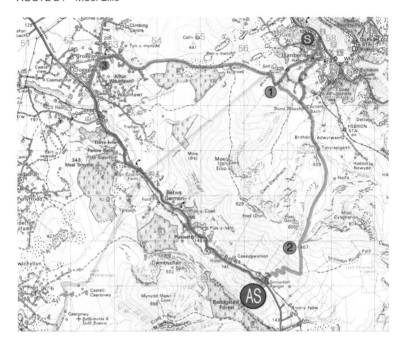

Gradient profile

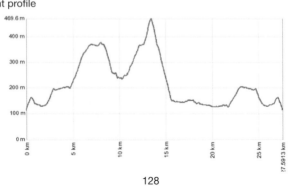

ROUTE 24 DETAILS - Moel Eilio

Length:	22km
Height gain:	600m
Difficulty:	Red
Commitment:	2
Stars:	★ ★
Map:	Explorer 17, Landranger 115

ROUTE SUMMARY

This route is a popular training run for those of us living in the Llanberis area, but it is also a very enjoyable XC ride particularly in the evening when the warm sunlight is glowing on the mountains and quarries. Late in the day is also better for getting a good run down the popular 'Snowdon Ranger' path, thick with walkers during the day. Some hard and technical climbing gives way to excellent descending and it rides well in both directions. The high-sided culverts either side of the Maesgwm section are a real pain causing untold numbers of punctures. If you can jump them then all well and good, otherwise caution is recommended.

Start from one of the lakeside carparks in Llanberis and make your way to Pete's Eats Café. From Pete's you have to negotiate the back roads of Llanberis; there isn't really an easy way around this so..... Head up the high street, pass Georgio's ice cream emporium then take the first right turn to climb up the narrow Snowdon Street to a T junction. Do a quick left then right shimmy before climbing up the next steep lane to another T junction where you do a quick right then left shimmy to climb out of the village and away.

The narrow road climbs ever more steeply to a ridiculous section just before a 'thank god' breather at a gate. Through the gate and on up until it is possible to take a left turn off the tar and onto a grassy track about 30m before the road-end carpark much used by paraglider pilots. Point 1. Follow this track with excellent views of the Dinorwig Quarries and the forbidden fruit of the quarry downhill ride. Reach another rough road at a gate, continuing along this as it heads into Maesgwm now with views of both Cloggy and Snowdon.

At GR 575 583 you reach the end of the road / track where the climbing returns in earnest as the trail narrows, steepens and becomes armour plated with stone blocks. Fight your way up this technical but entirely ridable climb (a good tick if you can do it) to a gate-enforced respite just beyond the hardest section. There is now a short smooth section before a long and physical climb up to the col, again this is entirely ridable but far from easy.

Point 2. At the col go through a gate then down a wide grassy trail to another gate some way off, descending quickly. The most rideable route is found by following the bridleway off slightly left (beware hidden ruts) where another trail goes straight on leading to a very steep and grassy section easily damaged and best avoided. Either

way you will soon hit the Snowdon Ranger path where you make a right turn down valley. You can actually ride legally to the summit of Snowdon by going left here, another day maybe... Drop down the path with a couple of very technical steps then smooth gravel interrupted by killer culverts to reach a farmhouse which you go behind. Cross the railway then go left along the path beside the station before dropping to reach the road at GR 564 550.

Turn right and settle in for an extended road session taking you as far as Waenfawr some 6km away. Climb into the village to take the second right turn up past the primary school at GR 527 593. Point 3. Climb again to the second (and more obvious) crossroads among the houses in Groeslon, go right up the dead straight, dead-end road just hoping that you have saved enough energy for another long climb. The views soon open up giving a good excuse to stop and look back over Caernarfon Bay to Llanddwyn Island at the mouth of the Menai Straits.

At the end of the road continue along the rocky track taking the right fork heading for a gate on the brow of the hill. The gate is the top of the last climb so kick back and enjoy the long, fast descent over the shoulder of Cefn-du ending in a rough section back to the road you fought up to get out of Llanberis. Point 1. The quickest way back is straight down; but if you have the energy it is more fun to take the right turn shortly after reaching the road to re-ride the track under Moel Eilio then take the next road left, steeply down past the campsite and YHA into Llanberis.

The start of the Maesgwm bridleway.

ROUTE 25 - Snowdon via Llanberis path

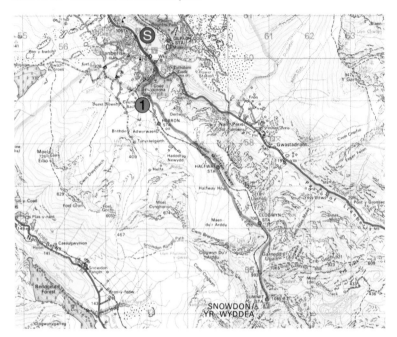

Gradient profile

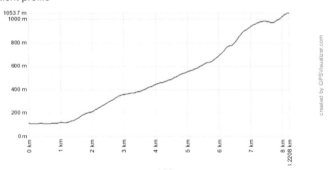

created by GPSVisualizer.com

ROUTE 25 DETAILS - Snowdon via Llanberis path

Length:	16km
Height gain:	1100m
Difficulty:	Black
Commitment:	3
Stars:	★ ★
Map:	Explorer 17, Landranger 115

ROUTE SUMMARY

Believe it or not there are three bridleways up Wales's highest mountain, the Rhyd-Ddu path, the Snowdon Ranger path and the Llanberis Path. The Llanberis is by far the most amenable but even that is a hard trip with an unrelenting ride / carry up and a very rough and technical descent. Between the 1st of May and the 30th of September riding is restricted to outside the hours of 10am and 5pm so most people do an evening trip, this can be a brilliant experience on a fine evening. Be sure to leave yourself plenty of light though, a two hour round trip is quick, you can double that without too much difficulty. Opinion is divided between those who think it is the best downhill trail in the UK and those who would rather rip

their own heads off than do it again. A 'double top' challenge taking in all three routes offers one of the hardest 35km (ish) rides on the planet. A triple top, ascending and descending all three routes would be something else entirely.

Start from one of the lakeside car parks in Llanberis heading up valley past the Snowdon railway terminus to take a right turn at the mini roundabout just beyond. Ride past Victoria Terrace and then get a good taste of things to come by fighting up the uber steep road beyond the cattle grid, there is a good café at the top of the hill.

The angle eases a little as you recover from the shock (and lack of warm up) passing some farm buildings and a

133

gate to reach the start of the bridleway proper at GR 581 589. Point 1. Go left onto this and begin the ride, carry, ride, carry, ride, carry game that continues for the next 8km. What the ratio of ride to carry is depends on your fitness, skill and bloody mindedness, 50:50 is good, enjoy. It is worth 'book-marking' some of the nasty bits for the way down. There is a good café at the top of the mountain.

If the café is open stay off the beer as the descent is just as much hard work as the climb, just differently so. Beware of Allt Goch the first really steep section off the summit, then the entry into Allt Moses just after the railway tunnel is nasty. The big steps down Allt Moses are rideable but tricky in the middle and unforgiving to land on. Things ease for a while past the halfway café but the last section is surprisingly hard and, as most people are pretty knackered by then, they tend to ride over stuff they would not normally attempt (stopping is just too much effort) leading to hard landings.

Back down the steep tarmac, the cafe, pub and physio await.

Ali 'The Stig' Chant rockin' in the evening sun, high on life and Snowdon.